# Village Swallows

ELIZABETH FRANCIS

NICHOLAS BALL

Printed Worldwide
First Printing 2022
First Edition 2022

ISBN: 978-0-9573465-2-9

Village
Swallows

# Table of Contents

# Village In A Valley

My village lies in a valley, and numbers 27 households, which include the ex-post office, the ex-shop, guest houses, and the hotel/village pub. Its name may have come from that of a 6th century Irish saint.

A river runs through it, just beside the winding narrow road, and the hills on either side are steep. One side of the valley is wooded, and the other has fields which rise to the moor. In autumn they show a purple rim, when the heather is out, and in winter the sun will turn the bracken to warm rich russet. In spring the fields are speckled white with young lambs, for this is hill-farming country and sheep are part of the landscape. Very picturesque, until they get loose and start roaming the village and eating our gardens.

The only ways into or out of the village involve one of four hills, but winter journeys can be quite hair-raising in icy weather. The valley runs from east to west, and the steppes of Russia could hardly seem colder when we are muffled against an east wind, scything its way between the houses.

"A mean wind, " Dave calls it. " "Too mean to go round you. 'Ee do go straight through instead."

The valley widens a little where we are, so the houses on the river side of the road mostly have very small gardens. Mine, I'm happy to say, is on the other side of the road and has a bigger one. In summer the sun streams down on us, pouring its rays into the bowl formed by the encircling hills. A south-facing garden in Devon, how enviably tropical that sounds!

All is not as lush as it sounds, however. This North Devon promontory rises and falls in tortuous by. The sea is not far distant, and although we live in a valley we are actually 750 feet above sea level. Mimosa trees outside are not for us.

Of the oldest inhabitants, in terms of tenure, not age, I have already moved up to number 4. The village looks so settled, when you gaze on it from the steep hillside on piggy corner, yet, in my time the post office changed hands 4 times, the shop 5 times and the pub has had 4 different owners. We have absorbed these shocks philosophically.

When the wife of one of the pub's owners fell foul of a local farmer blocking the road with his tractor he countered her wrath by enquiring how long she had been here.

"Three weeks, " was the haughty answer. "Move on."

"I 'ope you'll stay another three," said Tam, grinning broadly and staying put.

No matter how long one's tenure, there exists a "them" and "us" distinction. "Us" is everyone born locally, whose parents usually had grandparents and forebears going back for generations in farming. Old names still run like living threads among today's descendants. "Them" is people like me, who have bought properties and come into the area from outside. If we disagree with certain country practices we are immediately classed as townies; I don't think we will ever cease to be regarded as foreigners, however many years we stay, by the "us" fraternity. But one can achieve a kind of half-way status, and that is where I like to think I am.

Here I must speak up for the "incomers". We have bought many a run-down property amongst us, employed local labour, and restored houses to good and attractive homes. We have caused blind, broken windows to shine out in the dark again, junk yards and weed patches have become gardens, and all in all I think the valley has been visually improved since first I knew it.

Even the restoration work has its funny side. One building firm will remember Valerie! She was so keen and particular during the rebuilding of her ruined house that she was supposed to have stood over the men as they worked and dictated which stone went where. Before long, when told that the day's work was to be on her place, the whole workforce threatened to report sick.

Some of the farms and homesteads have names which are poetry. Larkbarrow, Cloud Farm, Tippacott, Lillycombe, Glenthorne.... What could be lovelier?

Speaking of ruins, one has a creepy memory for me. It is only the shell of a house now, and when I came upon it, while walking over the high and lonely moors, bright with heather, I suddenly heard what sounded like violins playing. I froze in my tracks. The cold wind lifted my hair... or was my hair beginning to stand on end? Shades of the court of Marie Antoinette claimed to have been seen in a ghostly vision by two women... I took a few fearful steps forward, and there behind a broken wall I saw... beehives!

I own a beehive now, also a dog, a cat, two idle hens and Harold, their lord and master, a large goat, and Ben, a pure-bred Exmoor pony. I didn't set out to acquire them, with the exception of the beehive I've always wanted to keep bees; they acquired me.

My cottage is curiously shaped, like a chopped-off wedge of cheese, and has a long garden of an equally odd shape. The river bustles along just across the road, and I have sat up in bed and watched a seagull catch a fish in it. I call it my Paradise, and though for many years I could only be here for weekends and holidays, now I live here all the time. In 13 years I haven't spent a night away from home, nor do I want to.

"Whatever will you do all day, in a place like that?" I was asked just before I came here permanently.

If I'm not up by seven, I won't get through all my day's activities. There are the chores, for even a small cottage gets dusty and acquires cobwebs, and things have to be washed. (Four feline paws make splendid patterns on a pale bedspread on a wet night.)

Then there is the garden, in which I grow nearly all my own vegetables. There are forty-mile round trips for major shopping safaris to local towns.

There are also the animals and various animal crises which sooner or later always seem to arrive at my door. A cat is missing; some wild kittens are found in a barn; cows get out; my goat has got rounded up with the sheep; a car won't start when a dog is due at the vets. Once I was asked if I could please come and give the cat her tablet, as Fluffy had spat it out three times.

Like Dr. Barnado, I could have a sign over the door; mine would read, " No animal crisis ever turned away." But I don’t think the sign is necessary, and I am told that one person has nicknamed me Mother Nature.

No, my days are not empty. The first hour is typically full. Get up and make a mug of coffee. Feed my cat, Sammie. Fill up the nut container for the birds. Hold out some crumbs for Robbie, the tame robin, to take from my hand. Go down the garden with coffee in one hand and Harold's bowl in the other. Let Harold and his ladies out and distribute their breakfast. Wander around the garden and look to see what has been nibbled or come out or blown over in the night. Finish coffee, and take the dog out.

We go up the road past the pub, across the footbridge over the river, and skirt the field to the path through the woods, wet or fine.

Usually, no-one else is about. The village is hardly awake yet, though curls of smoke show that Dave and Cyril, two other early risers, are stirring. Sometimes the eastern sky behind me is flaming in scarlet and gold, or soft in spring’s apricot and azure; sometimes I have been early enough to catch a moon and a paling star before the sunrise. A fox may cross my path, and grey squirrels chitter at Patch, who barks furiously at the base of their trees.

Her barks are likely to set off the Alsatian at one of the guest houses, the two dogs at the Old Mill, and the pair at the farm. If the village is not awake yet, it soon will be.

In the autumn I might climb up through the woods to get mushrooms in the top field. Here I can look down on the houses spread along the winding road like a toy village. Three new ones have been built in recent years, and four have been renovated and enlarged. One is a shack and an eyesore. Mine is one of the smallest cottages, with white walls, a new roof, and a crooked chimney which faithfully copies the old one it replaced.

How strange it is to look down on our little community and think that we are but the latest in the long line of people who have lived here. Men of the stone and bronze ages were before us.

The Romans and the Celts and the trading Phoenicians knew our coastline. We were once part of the kingdom of Wessex, and our cliffs were raided by the Danes. The Saxon Thane Odda defeated the Danish King Hubba in 878 A.D. on a site less than two miles from my mushroom field. (Surely this was one of the most beautiful of battlegrounds. On one side, huge, rounded hills sweep down into wooded combes; on the other, some of the highest cliffs in Britain drop into the blue-grey Bristol Channel, with the Welsh hills beyond. It can't have changed much to this very day.) From not far away, men sailed and fought against the Spanish Armada; when the Civil war raged, the nearest castle declared for the king and was the last stronghold of Royalism in the country. Hard-pressed fugitives could well have fled this way. What other eyes, long-closed, I wonder, have scanned this deep valley, as mine do now?

A tractor emerging from the farmyard jerks me back into the present and shows that Ron, who is a workaholic, is off on some venture or other, and a car inching across the field track tells me that Paul is probably taking his wife to work at the local hospital where she is a nurse. Soon a few more cars will appear, as people come down from the scattered houses along the far hillside to collect their morning newspapers from the pub. Another day is beginning, and it is time to go home for breakfast.

# Autumn

August is the beginning of autumn, no matter what the calendar says. Somewhere about mid-month, while having an early prowl around the garden, you experience the first real chill in the morning air. Something immensely far away and frozen has stirred and breathed out a reminder of snow and frost and ice.

Suddenly your eyes are opened. Yes, the rowan berries are no longer green, but tinted with orange. The morning dews are heavy and plants are beaded with cold drops. Spiders' webs are everywhere; later in the day you notice how the sun's angle has changed and lengthened the shadows - and how the evenings have drawn in. Gone are the magical long late twilights of summer.

Young robins abound and their wistful songs flute out constantly, mingling with the rippling music of the swallows. The swallows. . . ah, but where are the swifts? Gone already, slipping away while we were looking at the sweet peas and kidding ourselves that we had time in plenty. We always do. And there never is.

As early as August 17th I have seen a huge, excited gathering of swallows down the road at Lawn Farm. They line every telegraph wire and roof ridge, lifting, fluttering, settling again, and all the while twittering amongst themselves. Pass that way in an hour or two and the silence will be deafening. They've gone, and the empty air seems hollow in their wake.

In a few days, more will arrive from further afield, and perhaps crowd about my cottage. The same procedure is followed and the air of excitement is unmistakable. Every vantage point will be lined with birds, even small trees and shrubs, and then up and off they go, heading south in the great annual exodus at which I never cease to marvel. Such tiny birds to make so long a journey, each one no more than a heartbeat and a handful of feathers!

Once I was in Egypt at Christmas and had the totally unexpected sight of swallows skimming the Sacred Lake at Karnak. At least, I assume they were swallows, though they looked more brawny-coloured than our village ones. But there they were, dipping into the jade green water, and they made a special memory in an already memorable holiday.

I have seen groups of birds swirling and drifting overhead as late as October 14th, but our village ones have almost always gone by mid-September. Sometimes I miss the great event, and then the unaccustomed silence will tell me what has happened. Those rippling songs, so full of summer's joy, are gone for another six months.

The dates seem fairly consistent and have little to do with the onset early or late of cold weather. In 1986 I saw a very late little gathering on October 2nd, and the first frost was early, on October 16th. In 1997, the swallows were gathering on August 17th , and the first hard frost was not until late October. My diary has a note that in November 1988 the Bewick's swans were arriving in this country early from the Arctic, and this was said to presage a hard winter. In fact, it turned out to be the mildest one in a hundred years! So I don't attempt to relate the going of our little guests of summer to the kind of winter we may expect.

So often the autumn, which I count from August to November, can give us days of cloudless "Exmoor blue" skies and summer heat well into October. This blue seems to me to be peculiar to our part of the world. Just as northern France is said to have a bright quality of light all its own, so too we seem to get a shining radiance in our cloudless skies that is different from elsewhere. Perhaps this is due to the nearness of the Bristol Channel and the clean-swept moorland air. Or perhaps I'm just prejudiced!

The bright days may begin with mist, or glow into full light with dawns of rose and peachy gold. I call these "Dawn of the World" mornings, because they seem so perfect, each one a new and wonderful thing, when every flower and leaf will stand refreshed with dew. When the hot day is over, the garden flowers glow, almost luminous for a while, releasing pungent scents into the rapidly cooling air. A new moon may hang, a sliver of gold, in a sky of palest blue. The shadows deepen quickly now, but the afterglow lingers in dusky rose above black woods.

Clear nights can hold a million stars, brushed over with the faintly luminous sweep of the Milky Way. Orion reappears like an old friend over Lawn Farm, and shooting stars are numerous.

In contrast to the balmy weather, I have known the September air chilled and sharp on the hills, with racing skies of gold, cream, grey, and turquoise. Gales can fling us squalls of torrential rain, and hopes of a good mushroom harvest fade. Then the mood or the wind will change and chores must be scamped to catch another glorious day in the garden.

A sullen grey sea can change overnight to a tranquil thing of summer blue and green, with long white curls of breakers reflecting themselves glassily. One day a driftwood-collecting session on the beach can seem a sensible preparation for the winter fires; the next it is so hot as to be ridiculous, so one scuffs along the tide line instead and looks for things.

*The jar of sea glass pebbles*

What things? Bits of sea- polished blue and green glass, to drop into my collection in an old glass jar. When the sun shines through it, the colours sparkle prettily. I have not, as yet, found a piece of yellow glass and once when I thought I had, I inadvertently trod on a sea-weedy stone in my excitement, and sat down flat in the water. I then made a rapid retreat from the beach with wet pants and a red face.

September brings a peak in autumn's rich banquet of berries, nuts and fungi. This is a very good place for mushrooms, and when there is an especially good year one is spoilt for choice. Up in the top field they can grow in great swathes and circles and in no time at all the baskets are filled. Half-open, the white caps shine silky-smooth, and underneath, the wonderful pinky-beige ribs are just breaking free of their frill round the stem. No autumn pleasure is nicer than sliding one's fingers into the damp grass and twisting off each plant? Fruit? Vegetable? with delicate care. Their smell is the very essence of autumn, woody, mossy, with a faint edge of alluring decay.

Softened in butter and stirred into a white sauce, they can be folded inside savory pancakes for a delectable meal; the same mixture, with a pinch of thyme added, can be baked in a pie dish, lined and topped with pastry, for something more robust and equally delicious. But is anything better than simple mushrooms on toast for breakfast, when your appetite is sharp after your early morning foray?

In the middle of the second mushroom field grow some enormous specimens, and with these I once almost poisoned my friend Eva. I had picked big dark horse mushrooms before, from a corner of the field. These were slightly paler and grew right out in the open. I selected a bagful with great care and, Eva being out, I left them for her on her hall stand. Several days later I met her in the village shop and asked if she'd enjoyed them.

"Oh, it was you, was it?" she said gloomily. "Those weren't mushrooms. I wondered who was trying to poison me."

Happily, our friendship survived a day of intermittent stomachache and nausea. I learnt a lesson, though. Don't eat or give anything different unless it's first O.K.'d by a knowledgeable local.

My own autumn harvest from the garden is very rewarding. Six months of toil and care now yield (I hope) all my potatoes, onions and garlic to last until this time next year. I love inserting the fork, grasping the haulm, and levering up the first foremost spuds. In dry weather they come up clean and golden and I count the result eagerly. One year I got 110lbs. from a short row into which the compost heap had been dug, prior to planting the seed potatoes.

On another occasion I had an absolute disaster. The potatoes were contorted into hideous scabby shapes and looked like evil under-ground creatures. They didn't keep and went into a smelly squashy mess, and I tried to think what could have gone wrong. Then I remembered a hint in a garden magazine. "Plant your seed potatoes in grass cuttings, "it said. Whatever it is that attacks the spuds and causes scab would go for the grass instead. So I did. Oh, how those Nasties must have enjoyed themselves! They waxed lusty on the grass for starters, and moved on to my potatoes for their main course, and those vile knobby things were, I assume, the direct result.

I am always a bit wary of gardening hints now, and if one sounds interesting I try it in a small way first.

Gardeners' Delight tomatoes now ripen rapidly in my home-made tom house; runner beans usually keep me going until the first frost with tender perpetual spinach and Little Gem lettuce. Marrows come in too, and I hope to get a few to store until Christmas, after which they can get a bit stringy.

All the while I am going over my January King cabbages and sprouts and rubbing off butterfly eggs and caterpillars. How illogical we gardeners are! At one end of the garden I gaze at the buddleia Black Knight in rapture, as I count the red admirals, peacocks, painted ladies and tortoiseshells feasting tipsily there; at the other I am cussing and flicking at the cabbage whites as they hover over my winter greens.

I plant lettuce until early November, and cover each with a plastic bottle, minus cap and bottom. This keeps slugs and sparrows at bay, and when the lettuce is half-grown I take the bottle off and replace it with another cut into a cylinder, to give more room. Later plantings will have the bottles left on all winter. They grow very slowly then, but eventually reach a pickable size and give a tasty salad ingredient.

My lemonade bottles cause much amusement, but they work, and act as miniature greenhouses as well as slug-deterrents. My vegetable garden, when well-stocked with them, has been described as a lunar landscape.

Because the birds are so tame and numerous, after years of feeding, I am turning to more compact varieties of vegetables which are easier to cover. It is maddening to find pea haulms shredded to skeletons, and runner beans minus every flower. Next year (Ah, that ever-beckoning next year, when all will be magically transformed into straight rows of unblemished lushness!) Next year, I say, I shall try Pickwick runner beans, the Sutton broad beans, and the new Cavalier peas. And next year there will be no enormous teasel growing in the middle of the leeks. One must, of course, grow teasels for the goldfinches, but I shall stick them on the bank instead.

(Truth compels me to say that if the bank proves inhospitable, the teasels will be back among the vegetables again, tout de suite.)

The October flower garden can be one of the prettiest. My sheltered patch will still be bright with red kaffir lilies, fuchsias, michaelmas daisies, nasturtiums, mauve and white Japanese anemones, and the prolific yellow daisy with the ugly name of Argyranthemum. A hydrangea is getting going on the raised bed, after I nearly murdered it. I brought it home in luxuriant flowers from a garden center, and repotted it, shaking out the roots as I did so. Naturally, it wilted. Then a hot dry wind blew for three days and it wilted more. Autumn squalls followed, filling its tub, and it got water-logged. Seven pounds nearly went down the drain, but I nursed it in the sick bay, behind the raspberries, where it is cool and shady, and it forgave me and recovered.

Sometimes I squeeze in a tub of dahlias and chrysanthemums, but it is a squeeze. Much sleight of hand goes on in my small flower garden, and visitors will blink to find yesterday's lilies mysteriously transformed into today's gladioli. The pots are cunningly concealed by luxuriant foliage.

Planting the new season's bulbs is hazardous. One gingerly inserts a trowel, meets resistance, and draws out half a tulip. Curses! Why doesn't one mark them, before they die down completely? Try somewhere else, and heave a sigh of relief. In they go, daffodils and narcissi and crocus and aconites. I shall never see the latter again - either the mice eat them or they just don't like me. But still I go on planting them, fistfuls of cash, and I know that most things will reward me with gaiety and colour in the spring.

Meanwhile, on the moors, another flower garden is spread.

I could show you a little valley where the heather flings every shade of mauve and purple on all sides, right up to the green banks of a stream, where the rowan leans over, dripping with polished berries. Here my dog Rick, of beloved memory, had one of his selected bathing places, and would wallow and splurge in it to his heart's content. I know where a clump of pure white heather grows, and every year I Pick one sprig for luck. I call this quiet and beautiful place "God's Garden."

The edge of the wood is the place for sloes. Thick on the branches they are like unpolished jewels, rich with bloom. Next to them the hawthorns crowd their crimson berries and squirrels rustle after hazel nuts as I pick my yearly blackberries. None taste so winey as the wild ones.

On a crisp sunny morning, my early walk with Patch through the woods above the river will show me trees of copper and amber above waterfalls creaming into deep brown pools. The yellow leaves slip down on every puff of wind, casting down their golden crowns. I have one special beech tree, about fifteen feet tall, whose young branches are held in smooth symmetry all-round the grey trunk. When the leaves turn to their autumn yellow and the sun lights him up, I salute my "Little Prince", so fair in his rich clothing, regal and proud in his moment of glory.

But all is not ending and closing down in these autumn months.

The brown foxglove stems that I pick for my dried arrangements are packed with seeds, as was the honesty which I recently peeled in the garden. Likewise, the seedheads of hogweed, grasses and rushes, which all add height and grace, and which I always shake out before I bring them home. Nature will do the rest.

And there are new arrivals, too. Fieldfares and redwings have come to the autumn feast, and amongst the groups of finches I notice bramblings adding a smart flick of black and white. Now, a different music pipes where swallows sang.

# The Cottage

My cottage used to belong to two old ladies who, I was told, lived on a bottle of sherry a day and were always asking passers-by what day it was. They had caught the kitchen on fire and so when I first saw it, it was coal-black and much charred where their cooker had been. A large barn was built onto the back of the house, into which the kitchen window opened, so it was hellishly dark.

There is a long sitting room behind the kitchen, and upstairs

are two bedrooms and the tiniest loo ever seen, built in what might have been a cupboard. But it is big enough to hold a bath and an ancient you-know-what, and when I replaced these items I was able to squeeze in a small wash basin. But I am rushing ahead.

I came to see the cottage with a surveyor, who had been contacted for me by my solicitor. Together we tramped all over it. and he insisted that I climbed up into the loft to see the rafters.

"They don't build roofs like this nowadays," he said, almost caressing the great beams.

Outside we forced our way through a tangle of hawthorns and weeds, looking for the septic tank, whose whereabouts would probably be marked by luxuriant nettles. Our search was shortened by Margie, the nicest neighbour I have ever had, who came and pointed out the spot.

"I can't mistake it, "she said, indicating as well her five-year-old son. "When they came to clear it out, Stuart fell in it."

(Stuart later became my constant companion. "I'll hell up you," he would say, chopping the heads off emerging daffodils during a weeding session.)

The deeds were signed, some weeks later, in a pub car park some forty miles away. There was a postal strike at the time, and this was the only way we could short-circuit things between current owner and impatient buyer. I spent one of my happiest Easter holidays scrubbing my little dolls' house from top to bottom with Sunlight soap. The blackened kitchen took me three whole days to clean. Margie's two cats, Nobby and Tuppence, obligingly ate all the dead flies on the windowsills for me.

Stuart's insistence on helping often led him to arrive before eight o'clock in the morning, if he could give his mother the slip. I would see the bobble on his knitted hat appear over the edge of the small square window set into the back door, and have to drop out of sight to all fours, with the tea and biscuits which I was just taking back to bed. The floor was cold stone, so one wished to hurry, but one's house coat was long and tangled one's feet causing more than one mishap with the tea and biscuit.

Few are more persistent than a lively five-year-old. I gave in at last over another matter, which was to have him to lunch. His menu selected (fish and chips, peas and carrots, followed by ice cream). I told him not to come before twelve o'clock. Just after eight, sitting up in bed with my tea, I overheard the following from the front porch.

"Hello, Stuart. Whatever are you doing. Sitting down there?"
"I'm going to lunch. "

"But it's not breakfast time yet."

"I know. She won't get up."

On another occasion. I ignored all the raps on the door, only to find, sometime later, a very small and gritty trout laid on the step. It was the first he had ever caught, and I felt rather mean.

Incidentally, I am amazed – looking back – that once I could stay in bed until eight o'clock! It has now become seven at the latest for getting-up time, which just goes to show how full my country life has become.

To return to the cottage.

My first priority was to remove the barn and let in the daylight, which I did with the magnificent help of a kind friend.

What I mean is, he did it and I helped. The sheets of rusty corrugated iron were removed by a farmer to repair his pigsty, and I sawed up all the wood for my evening fires.

The rendering on the house wall was then revealed, in a dubious state, and during my summer holiday I had another blissful time hacking it off where it was 'blown', and re-rendering it with cement. I had never done anything like this before, but half the secret of DIY is confidence. I asked around, and read books, and I am proud to say that my handiwork is sound to this day, except for one bit that I recently made good again… after well-over twenty years.

How delighted I was when the great day came to paint the wall white! In those days I wasn't very happy up ladders (practice has remedied that), but slowly and cautiously I did it, and when I had finished, my clothes went straight into rubbish bag as they were more white than colored. For some reason, butterflies loved the paint I used, and as it dried they collected on it, slowly fanning their wings in apparent ecstasy. Often I have paused to study a beautiful peacock's wings, inches from my nose, my brush drooping, which is how a lot of the paint got on to me instead of the wall.

My next job was to take down the old plaster ceiling in the smaller bedroom, because a large piece of it had fallen away. Have you ever taken down an old plaster ceiling? If so, you will know why it was that my friend and I looked like Abominable Snowmen at the end of the day. We wore sunglasses to keep the dust out of our eyes. We wore old hats, with handkerchiefs tied gangster-fashion over our mouths. I hung a sheet over the door, but even so, we ate, sniffed, blinked, and trod white dust. But we did it, and between us we put up a new plasterboard ceiling. Shortly after it was finished, I walked into the room and saw a foot dangling through it. I should have had the wiring in the loft sorted out first.

As a little light relief from all this heavy stuff, I think the garden got tackled next. What a training ground for jungle war fare it would have made! Hawthorn, elder, sloes, rosebay willow herb, ground elder, nettles…you name it, I had it. But underneath, how beautiful the earth was, rich and dark as fruit cake, and it has grown steadily richer with each year's compost. The only stony patch was where the barn stood, but I prised them all out eventually and made my flower garden there.

As soon as possible I turned my attention to the sitting room. It always smelt musty, and no wonder. Nine layers of wallpaper had to be scraped off. I wish I could have preserved the last one, which was old and of an interesting green and white feather design, with traces of a quaint frieze of Victorian figures. But it had to go and at last I stood knee-deep in paper, at which point the local vicar called. And stayed.

One day, Valerie came in when I was gazing in satisfaction at the walls, newly covered in a rough-textured paper and painted white. The ceiling was newly white too. This is of plasterboard, held with long battens which crisscross and make a pattern of squares. I think it is attractive, but not so Valerie. For her, the plasterboard and battens would have had to be removed. She reached up and tapped.

"Have you beams?" she enquired sharply.

I humbly admitted that I knew not what was on the other side. However, I passed the test in the kitchen, as here there is a beam, and the plaster ceiling has ancient hooks in it, for hanging thing on.

But I sinned when I painted he beam black. Valerie bought old beams from a barn for her house and left them in their natural state, wormholes, cracks and all.

In due course, I began to refurbish the loo, in which I have had no less than three new baths. My apparent passion for new baths is explained by the fact that two of them came to grief. It happened like this.

Strolling through a showroom near where I then worked, I one day saw a summer sale offer. Loo, cistern, bath and washbasin, all for less than £100, and in a pretty shade of green. I arranged to have a smaller washbasin substituted, and collected the lot to bring down to Devon at the weekend. Of course I was careful with It – who wouldn't be? and it travelled without mishap. My plumber removed the old items and installed the new, contorting himself marvelously to work in the confined space.

A couple of months later, I was cleaning the bath when my sponge snagged on something. A little tongue of the green shiny surface had sprung away from the fiberglass backing. A long battle with the suppliers then ensued. I must have bashed it en route, I was told. The plumber had whacked it. Our baths have always been satisfactory, our Mr. So and So, with whom you dealt, is on holiday. And so it went on, but I don't give up easily, and finally I think they got fed up with my visits and agreed to replace it.

Bath number two, also of fiberglass, went down to Devon wrapped up in all the old blankets I could muster. It was laid upon cushions and wedged in place by pillows. Tablecloths tenderly protected its surface, and no royal baby could have been given a smoother journey. It was fitted, and all was well. Until someone tripped over the bathmat and fell into it, hitting the bottom with the hand that wore a large heavy watch.

Out came that one, with the hole right through it. My insurance covered the cost, but on the advice of the plumber (who said he could see I was bath buggered), I added some extra cash and got one of pressed steel instead of fiberglass. I recommend anyone else to do the same.

Of course, the ideal way to tackle a property on which there is a fair amount to be done is to start at the top and work downwards, but this can't always be arranged. Little things like time and money intrude. My cottage was renovated a bit at a time, first to make it clean and comfortable, and then to improve it.

So it came about that the fireplace in the sitting room was not altered until long after the room was decorated. There just wasn't the time. It irritated me, because it was a modern one of beige tiles the sort you used to see in hundreds of houses - and totally out of keeping with the high overmantel, with its two shelves, into which it was set.

I painted these black (to Valerie's dismay), and decided that until I had the time to take the fireplace out it might look better without the tiles. One or two were cracked and a few were loose, so I started to prise them off. The plain base looked encouraging, so I went to work enthusiastically and soon had quite a little heap of tiles.

I lent the cottage to some friends at this time, for a few days, and when I came down on the Friday evening I found a present of a pottery jar of honey waiting for me, together with a very appreciative note. The note ended with the words, "By the way, Don has stuck all your fireplace tiles on for you."

Eventually the day came when could take the whole thing out. I was a little apprehensive, in case the wall fell down with it, but I got the hearth levered up first and then gingerly hacked a hole so that I could insert a crowbar behind the upright part. Heave and tug… heave and tug… and suddenly it came away. A neighbour helped me to carry it out into the garden, where it was later broken up and taken to the local tip. And what was then revealed?

Traces of an old, rough stone fireplace, just what I had visualized. It needed scraping and chipping clean of cement, and some of the stones were crumbling and had to be eased out and replaced with matching ones. I used to drive round the lanes slowly, peering at the banks for oblong or square ones, or long thin ones, and great was my pleasure when the chosen one was trimmed and made to fit into its place.

After the sides were made good – and how good they looked to me, after that nasty cheap tiled affair – I had to buy and fit a fireback and a hood. The fireback was easily found at a builders' merchant.

I became quite attached to builders' merchants. They were always filled with large purposeful men in dungarees, all asking at the counters for the most extraordinary things. Very interesting conversations could be overheard.

Salesman to Dungarees: "You next?"

Dungarees: "Ar. Alf dozen one-inch copper six foot."

Salesman (leaning backwards and calling into a small hatch):

"Bert! Copper one inch six foot?"

Voice off: "Not till termorrer. Lorry's broke down."

Dungarees: "Bloody 'ell."

Then he would turn round and see me, the only woman in a queue of broadly grinning men and go puce.

Mysterious and grubby bits of paper would be passed across the counter, rarely any money, and I felt that I had become a member of a very masculine club. They all knew the passwords for obtaining their requirements; I often had to describe the things I wanted, sometimes causing amusement, but always finding willing help and advice.

The hood over the fireplace, correctly called, I think, a canopy, was found in a junk yard. I became almost as fond of these as I was of builders' merchants. All the new canopies I had been shown were of copper, and very, very expensive. Mine cost me £2 (when we had real money) and looked just right when the rust was cleaned off and it was painted matt black.

*The fireplace remains unchanged*

A thick rough wooden plank, found on the beach, was fixed over the fireplace, where the stones met the white wall. It, too, was painted… guess what?

Finding the flat stones for the hearth was easy, and soon my fireplace was finished. Many is the cheerful blaze it has held, and visitors always love to put on the logs and watch the green and blue and orange flames leap up. A real fire has a life and soul of its own, and is a companion in the cool of the evening and the chill of winter.

By degrees, other improvements were made. The emulsion paint on the walls in the kitchen and loo flaked, after a while, so the walls were panelled and given a coat of gloss paint. This was a tedious job, but worth it.

First, holes had to be drilled so that wooden blocks could be fixed to the walls. In places the plaster was so soft that it poured out in a stream of red dust. This meant cleaning out a hole and filling it with cement, to provide a firm anchorage for the rawl plugs. Once all the blocks were in place, wooden battens were fixed on them, from floor to ceiling. On to these the panels of hardboard were screwed.

A kind builder acquaintance told me and my helper to throw water over the panels first – I supposed to allow for any shrinkage. Once dry, the rough side was given a coat of aluminium paint to seal it. When the panels were up, they took a coat of emulsion paint, undercoat, and gloss paint beautifully, and the work is good and sound to this day – a great improvement. The kind friend who did all this with me was the one who fell into the bath, so his sins were forgiven him.

Our local builder was ever helpful – dear Will. He viewed some of my handiwork with cement and announced with a twinkle that he would have to watch out, or I should be setting up in opposition and putting him out of business. Will is remembered every spring, as before he died he gave me some tulip bulbs which came up for him every year without fail. They do the same for me, and I always call them Will's tulips.

Rod, another builder, put me a new roof, chimney, and three new windows in the rear of the cottage. I got a generous grant for all this work, and for the loft insulation, and my only worry was that the garden would be wrecked while all the work was going on. I need not have worried. So quick, clean and careful was Rod and his little team, that I couldn't even find a broken leaf. He did the job one February, when the sun poured down and cups of tea and coffee could be taken into the garden. They used to sit there enjoying the vivid colours of all the crocus, the carpet of snowdrops, and the luminous green of a large Helleborus Corsicus, one of my favourite plants.

Rod also told me off for hanging a bag of nuts close against the landing window.

"No wonder the sill was rotten," he said. "Bird lime is powerful stuff. We'll have no more nuts on the window if you please."

There are many snags and worries to having a weekend cottage, apart from the security aspect.

Snow fell and melted suddenly in April one year, and kind neighbours came and put buckets to catch the drips. (That was before I had the new roof,) Even so, my bed was soaked. Condensation built up and made mildew on the ceilings as the cottage heated and cooled again each weekend. Once, the river flooded halfway across the road and the police advised me to hurry my departure on the Sunday afternoon, in case there were more floods on the way and I would have to make long detours. I piled blankets and rugs against the doors and someone put sandbags outside but I left with anguish in my heart.

All was well, though. Our river has a very rapid rise and fall, and by the time I arrived at the other end the phone was ringing with the welcome news that the flood had subsided.

Now I live here all the time and worries like that are a thing of the past. My little cottage is now cosy with central heating, clean and trim inside and out. It has not been tarted up with fitted this, that, and the other. It is pretty and homely and it seems to say, "Welcome", when you walk in. A tiny piece of ground has been bought to square off my vegetable garden. The birds flock to their bird table and the air is full of their lively chatter and cheerful songs.

"You know," said one visitor "you live in Paradise."

I think so, too.

# Chimney Sweep

Two or three times a year I get out my rods and brushes and sweep the chimney. For some reason, I positively enjoy doing it. Perhaps it takes me back to childhood days, when "getting the sweep" was an event. I can still remember his name - Mr. Osgood - and he rode a bicycle to which was attached a home-made trailer for the soot. His wife, having no garden at their tiny house, treated herself to florists' flowers, and my mother and I always looked forward to seeing the beautiful display in her porch when we went to book her husband's services.

The sweep who comes to houses in the village arrives in smart overalls and drives a posh van. He has a suction contraption which goes up the chimney, and the last neighbour I spoke to about it said that the job took less than ten minutes, for which she had to pay £10.

Sweeping my chimney takes me less than an hour, and this includes covering the mantelpiece, removing the rug, putting newspaper over the nearest shelves, clearing up afterwards, and washing my clothes. I always know when it is time to do the job because bits of soot start falling down onto the fire. Two or three times I have left it a bit too late and caught the chimney alight - not to the point where flames leapt from the top, but enough to cause clouds of smoke to roll down the village street and heads to protrude from windows. When this happens, I rake out the fire, keep my fingers crossed, and sweep the chimney the very next day.

When the due time arrives, I am up at six sharp. Out comes the brush from its hook in the garden shed, and outcome the rods from the back of the cupboard under the stairs. It takes ten of them to get the brush right up and poking out of the chimney pot. This still looks faintly ridiculous to me, and as a child it always made me laugh, when the sweep sent me out to look. You must always keep twisting the rods to the right, otherwise the action of waggling the brush about in the chimney could cause them to unscrew, and hey presto! Some of them will come down, but the rest will be left behind, stuck up there with the brush.

This reminds me of the day when I offered to sweep someone else's chimney.

Alas, I found it was too small for the proper brush and rods, so I rigged up a smaller affair, using a household brush which was designed for dust and cobweb removal from ceilings, and lengths of garden cane.

The chimney was actually a flu pipe from a wood burning stove and unknown to me it only went part of the way up inside the huge old stone chimney. I got my home-made effort up there all right, but when I tried to pull it down again, the brush got stuck on the edge of the metal flu pipe and wouldn't budge. I had tied it to the canes with long lengths of baler twine, so that one end of the line was in my hand, but pull and waggle as I might, there was no movement aloft. That is, until I gave an extra strong yank, and the baler twine frayed against the rim of the pipe. Down came the canes, and left the brush and its wire handle behind.

It was a beautiful day, that day… one of those hot, cloudless ones when the sky is deep blue and the breeze is just enough to make sitting in the garden with a book sheer bliss. I kept thinking about it as I spent hour after hour trying one way and another to get that beastly brush down. In the end I rang up the local fire officer, told him what had happened, and asked if it would be safe to leave the brush up there, as it wasn't very big.

"Oh, yes, " he said cheerfully. "It will singe itself away, probably. Is this the first time you've tried to sweep your chimney?"

"No", I said bitterly. "I've done my own for years. This is a neighbour's."

"Oh, bad luck, "he said, roaring with laughter as he rang off. Worse was to follow. I was, by this time, completely covered in soot. The scarf had long since slipped off my head, so hair, ears, face, neck, hands and clothes were black. Puffs of soot even came out of my shoes when I walked. My neighbour agreed, on the fire officer's advice, to leave the brush where it was and call it a day. I only had one desire - to nip across the intervening garden, strip everything off, and begin the first of several baths.

I hastened out - and walked slap into Rod, my builder. He had come to set up his scaffolding next door, prior to starting a roof repair.

We both stopped dead. His eyes seemed to bulge. He didn't say a word. Then he averted his gaze, turned his head away, and walked on. But not before I had seen him go bright red with the laughter which he was trying not to let out. As I fled inside my garden, I caught a glimpse of him leaning against his ladder, head bowed on to folded arms, and shoulders shaking wildly.

That was my first attempt at sweeping someone else's chimney. It was also my last.

# The Animals

When I first had the cottage I used to bring a guinea pig to and fro with me. My interest in guinea pigs arose from having looked after Toddles for a time, and becoming attached to him. On his decease, not feeling that my busy life permitted me to have a cat or dog, I went out and bought another one and called it Mo. As I left the pet shop, the owner said, "It's a girl, by the way."

Mo took to a travelling life, and became equally as tame as Toddles. I could leave her busily munching in the garden on her own for an hour, and she would come at a call. Mo began to look rather large, and one evening during the week, at the other house, I heard faint squeaks coming from her hutch.

Mo was not as innocent as her gentle manner and calm eyes had seemed to suggest when I bought her. There had been Goings On, and she produced twins. So now there were three. Alice and Rupert also took to travelling, but once I had ascertained that Rupert was a gentleman (of sorts), he had to have an apartment of his own. They travelled in large cardboard boxes, and on arrival at the cottage one weekend Rupert's box was empty. He gazed up at me from the wrong one, Alice and Mo on either side of him.

I didn't think Alice was old enough to reproduce, but I worried for some time about Mo. This was during the period when Britain was struggling with strikes towards the end of Edward Heath's administrator. One evening I had just gone into the dining room, at the other house, when the door flew open.

"Heath has just declared a three-day working week, there are going to be power cuts, and Alice has just had twins, said a friend who had stayed to tea.

So, Alice begat Scruffy and Lucy, and now there were five. And in no time at all, Rupert did it again, and then there were seven. Loading their boxes every weekend in addition to suitcases and groceries became rather a chore, so I decided to leave them behind.

Large and expensive drip-feed water bottles were purchased for each cage, together with sumptuous well-hearted cabbages. Their dishes were piled with their special dry food. Then I thought of fire and break-ins… and the little flock travelled as usual. I often made pens in the garden and took them all out on the grass for the afternoon, which they greatly enjoyed. They are delightful little animals and respond intelligently to affectionate care. But in due course, they were no more, and the guinea pig era was over.

Meanwhile, another era had dawned. The cats began to arrive. The first one to call at the cottage was a very nervous black and white one. He slipped along the hedges every day from a near-by farm, to have his saucer of milk and plate of food. Gradually I gained his confidence and christened him Flea. I always left him a large pile of macaroni cheese, to which he was partial, when I left on Sundays. Then I was told that during my absence Flea was meowing for me. I found an obliging lad, offered pocket money, left tins of catfood and Ideal milk, and a box in the porch, and felt that his needs were catered for. Flea stayed.

The next on the scene was Hoover, a large tabby.

"Is it a female?" asked Eva. "Because if so, you'll get kittens."

She was, and I did. More tins of catfood, more boxes in the porch which were soon piled up like high-rise flats. The kittens were sweet, though. They whizzed about the garden, and what one did they all did. I wished I'd had a camera at the ready when they all dug their little holes and sat in a solemn row, "obliging."

A home was offered to Tim, one of the kittens, by some nice holiday makers who Lived in Essex. I knew them quite well and was satisfied as to suitability, where animals were concerned, (always a heart-searching affair), and arranged for Tim to be collected. He and his mother pushed off all that day, and only re-appeared when his would-be owners had gone home. Clearly, Tim did not wish to go to Essex, so he stayed. So did Jassy, a pretty little tortoiseshell. The third kitten went to someone else, but it did not live very long, and neither did Jassy. I think that Hoover was perhaps coming to the end of her ability to produce robust families, although Tim was luckier.

That left me with three cats, and before long Tim brought home a wife. Dear little Mrs. Tim! She lived for many years and was the most devoted of cats. She had beautiful emerald green eyes, which Tim obviously found irresistible, because Primrose and her sister arrived in no time at all, after which both Hoover and Mrs. Tim were "arranged" by the vet.

I kept Primrose, also "arranged" when old enough; she was another tortoiseshell, and one of the prettiest cats I've ever seen. Her sister went to a lovely home, and was christened Lucky, and Primrose travelled to and fro with me every week and gradually became known as Gertie. She was a little devil for trying to stay out at night, and catching Gertie became one of my nightly and exhausting tasks. She loved it, and the game became lengthier and lengthier. I was heart-broken when she was killed on the road.

It was after this that Mrs. Tim became my shadow. Who says animals don't know and share our feelings?

She too was a tabby, with rather prim and old-maidish ways, but twice a year she would go off on a rave-up, in spite of having been "arranged". Down the garden she would go, calling for the toms, and disappear for three days. I was nearly sick with worry until I got used to the routine.

First, she would hold court under a wood pile in a near-by field. There they would sit motionless for hours; I couldn't see much fun in that for anybody, least of all the toms. Things warmed up a bit when phase two started and Mrs. Tim moved to an adjacent hedge. Yowlings and fights would begin and carry on throughout the night. Lastly, the gang followed her to the pub fire escape, and I at last got a glimpse of her suitors. A more raggedy and bent-eared lot it would be hard to find; these were the real mobsters, never seen by day unless lured out by a female. Mrs. Tim might have had prim ways normally, but she certainly attracted the roughs and toughs on these occasions.

She got cornered by a large tabby tom belonging to Irene, who lives a quarter of a mile away. He made the journey to Mrs. Tim, and didn't stand any nonsense. He grabbed her and started to give her the works, and she yelled blue murder. Up the garden she streaked, spitting and swearing, and that was the end of that rave-up. She then followed her usual procedure and ate a large meal, drank well, and toddled upstairs to sleep it off for hours under my bed.

"You are a disgusting little tart," I would tell her, lifting up the valance to look at her. A paw would stretch lazily out, and the beautiful emerald eyes would blink heavily.

Did she murmur, "Ah, but it was worth it?

Alongside these residents was a string of ginger visitors, known as First, Second, Third, and Fourth. First eventually stayed, and lived out his allotted span; Second – a beautiful rich amber colour – came daily for a long time, and then ceased to visit. Ages afterwards I think I traced him; he was found dead in a neighbour's garden, and we think he picked up some poison. Third stayed around for some time and then went off for a year, to reappear slimmer but in perfect condition. As he was apt to spray the air on the whim of the moment, I was not entirely dismayed when he pushed off again.

Fourth caused me much amusement. He had a hearty appetite and would run up the garden mewing plaintively, so - although he was quite sturdy - I used to pile up his plate end tell the lad, Dougal, to leave him plenty in my absence. He liked to sleep it off in a tiny breadbasket on the freezer top, into which he could only squeeze two legs. Everything else overflowed. His golden eyes would blink down at me with a dopey expression, and one day I fetched Nan, the current owner of the village shop, to see him.

"Fourth can go anywhere in the house that he likes," I said, "but look at him! He can't be comfortable!"

She let out a shriek. "Fourth? That's our Donnie! You're paying Dougal to feed his Own cat!"

Artful Donnie wasn't so dopey after all.

And so it went on. They came and they went over the years, and I made a cat flap in the kitchen door so that they should have that much more shelter in the winter. Born under the hedges, because the farmers won't have the adults spayed or neutered, they were nobody's cats, and I loved them all.

When I came to live here permanently, I had four residents- Mrs. Tim, Ginger, Blacks, and Sammie.

Blacks was so wild when he turned up that he lived for a year down the garden in a little wooden house that I made for him. Slowly he became tame and came into the house for his meals. When I was stroking Ginger (who usually fell over in ecstasy), Blacks would take a swipe at me, and I guessed that he was trying to pull my hand towards him for stroking purposes. As he never learnt to sheathe his claws, it was some time before I risked touching him, so he used to weave round the table legs, but eventually I risked it, and he soon became a regular softie and a devoted friend.

Sammie was dumped in the village when he was about six months old. He was a perky ginger and white, and I was upset when I heard him crying outside Valerie's house, on a wet November night, and she wouldn't do anything for him. I had only just arrived for the weekend, and had looked in to see her. If she wanted a cat, she said, she would get a proper cat, not a stray. I left my coffee half drunk and walked out, picked up the little scrap, and brought him home, and a rift was made which never quite healed afterwards.

What a joy Sammie has been! Full of mischief, clean indoors from the very first, even though he had to be nursed through dysentery. He would lie quietly on lap and then suddenly fly up at buttons, or a tie, and fight them furiously. Several unsuspecting guests sat thus with him, peacefully reading the paper, and then I would hear a sudden yell, and know that he had startled them to death.

He also had a trick of flashing in under the bedclothes as one made the bed, and it wasn't until you went to smooth out the lump that you found it was Sammie, who at once shot up and down like an eel, except that he had four legs going like pistons to try and catch your hand and start a fight.

I went into the garden one morning to find that he had contorted himself into the bird table and was hanging over the dangling nut container with a look that plainly said, "Now come and get 'em!"

*The bird table*

My kind and skillful vet helped him to get over yellow jaundice, when his skin was as yellow as a canary, kidney trouble, and later a kind of semi-permanent asthma. None of this dimmed his joy of living for long. We still go for walks together around the fields beyond the garden. He got used to this when he was getting over the kidney trouble and I was told that if he caught anything while out (he's a terrible hunter), I must try to see that he didn't eat it. The only way to do this was to go with him, which I did; we used to walk along Mouse Bank and there I would sit while he hunted. I felt that I was becoming quite an expert mouser myself, through watching him, but I didn't actually come running home with one in my mouth!

He is now the last cat left. Any other waifs and strays will be passed to good animal rescue places, because as I get older the anguish of inevitable parting seems to get worse.

Then there was the dog episode.

Somewhere about the time that Mrs. Tim arrived, a friendly (and hungry) dog from a local farm took to sitting on my doorstep. How can one not give them food, when their eyes beseech and they are obviously underfed? He would chase after the car when I left on Sundays, and welcome me back with joy on Friday nights. Enquiries revealed that his owner had ceased active farming and was often away. He left a pile of dog meal tipped out in a shed, I was told, so no wonder the dog scavenged and fought.

With hindsight, I wouldn't advise any compassionate person to go and live in the country unless you are prepared for heartaches. I worried sorely over this dog. Then, one day, his owner came to see me. He said that he had to go away for a week and would I like to look after the dog? I at once said that I would love to give him a permanent home, but the man mumbled and muttered in a typical North Devon local's way and I couldn't get a straight answer out of him. Off he went – and I didn't see him again for five months.

Now, of course, there was a real problem. How could the dog be expected to go back to his old life of hungry neglect, when he had lived in the lap of luxury? I lost nearly a stone in weight during that period. Then the owner turned up again, and I begged to keep the dog.

"Oh, well," he said at least, "he'd better stop here. But don't give him to anyone else."

I was overjoyed. I christened him Rick, and rushed off to buy a dog license. A week later the wretched man slowed down in his car as he passed me, with Rick on a lead after we'd had a long walk.

"I shall have to have him back one day, you know," he said.

The bottom fell out of my world. I felt sick with apprehension. Then I swore to myself that nothing would make me relinquish the dog to this devious old devil, who, I later found out, had the reputation for being one of the cruelest men on Exmoor where live-stock were concerned. A lad told me that he had a pit where he threw dead sheep, which sometimes weren't quite dead when he did so. I can believe it. You should have seen Rick cower at first when you picked up a stick, until he learnt that he was safe.

In due course, the man sent his son down to see me. I was out, but a neighbour intercepted him and sent him off with a flea in his ear, together with a few hard facts about the dog's neglect.

Presently I received a solicitor's letter, telling me to hand the dog in at the local police station on a certain date. Did I hell! I had previously written to the man and offered to buy Rick, at his own price, so now I went to a solicitor and told the whole story.

"Don t worry," he reassured me. "You'll be laughing over the teacups about this in a year's time. We'll start by sending him in a bill for the dog's keep when he left him with you for five months."

Well, to cut it short, eventually I got Rick for £50, and his legal costs, and I would still have rejoiced if I'd been charged £500. At last I slept peacefully at nights. Rick, who was a black and white border collie, lived for many happy years. He learnt to play, and respected the cats, and was never more delighted than when sitting on the front seat of the car and sailing off for an outing. I always took him to work with me, and he was as good as gold.

My vet had to ease him out, when he eventually developed Leukemia, but between us we kept him going until he was no longer comfortable.

"Never another dog," I vowed then.

As I write this, I can see out of the corner of my eye a recumbent figure on the settee, with a black patch over one eye, a rough coat, and a longish tail which, at the moment, is not wagging.

Patch came to live near me four or five years ago. I looked after her several times when her owners went away, and I gathered that although she had been a boy's pet and slept on his bed, she was gradually relegated to the garden shed as he grew up. She also had to share it with a slobbering bloodhound, which was number one favourite after it arrived. On the last occasion when I looked after her she didn't want to go home.

One Sunday lunch time, out of the blue, I was told," We're going to get rid of Patch. I suppose you wouldn't have her?"

What could I do?

Shortly afterwards, in she bustled, and her lead was thrown over the fence after her. She had no toys, no blanket, nothing of her own to bring... but did she care? I had an animal's basket up in the loft, a couple of blankets came out of the blanket box, and that dog went happily upstairs to bed that night, with several biscuits to keep her company.

She had been taught to chase my ginger and white Sammie, but once I had told her No, she never attempted to do so again, and now they sit side by side in perfect harmony. She is a dear dog, loving her walks and rides, with a weakness for tea and biscuits. I hope I shall have her for a long time yet.

I haven't had much to do with horses until the last few years or so. Then I became aware of two who lived all the year in one or other of two fields along the river. I began to take them a few biscuits in my pocket, and soon this was a regular event. They waited for me at their gate, so I had to go and see them with a treat every day.

One was a stocky little chap, tan and beige, with a flowing mane and tail, and glorious eyelashes. He would get bits of fern or hawthorn tangled between his ears, and sometimes he looked quite bridal. I called him Squealie, because of his shrill neigh when he saw me coming. The other one was bigger, slim and dark brown, and I called this one Browns, and referred to them both as "my boys."

Presently I met their owner. He had rescued them both from poor circumstances, and although I think it was a bit of a struggle at that time, he kept them going in the winter with hay and left—over items from a vegetable shop. I asked if I might help my boys out in the cold weather with soaked sugar beet pellets, and he was delighted.

He also pointed out that Browns was a mare.

Two years ago there was an emergency when a farm was sold and Bessie and Boddie, to give them their proper names. Had to be moved I knew someone who let them use a small field, and helped to take them up there. I visited them every day and my heart ached for them in the bitter weather, because they had little shelter. I used to wake in the night and hear the sleet hissing down on the window and think of them up there in the cold and dark, and worry about them.

Further enquiries found a nearer neighbour who had a paddock and empty stabling, so "my boys" came home to the village and were delighted with their winter accommodation. I loved leading Bessie home. She wouldn't budge until Boddie was led in front of her, and then we all processed in fine style.

Then I had another pair of horses to worry over, one of which was Ned, now my own Exmoor pony. He lived in a field locally with a big old white horse called Topper. There was stabling available, but they were looked after very erratically. Sometimes they would be inside for two or three bitter nights, and left out for the next few. And sometimes, when they were in, they would be forgotten and left there all day with little food and water - and occasionally, none. In summer they would stand patiently at the gate, waiting for water.

In the middle of a bad patch of very windy wet weather, Topper and Ned got out and disappeared. When on the loose, they always made for a certain hill, but for six days no-one knew where they were.

Then someone knocked at my door and said he'd seen them two or three miles away near, the boundary between Devon and Somerset. I dived into a mac and wellies, found their owner, and we set off by car in search of them. It was blowing a gale and raining hard still, and to my dismay the casual search was quickly abandoned. The next day, the same thing happened, and this time I said that I would ride to the top road, and then, I was going on foot to find them.

We sew them on the horizon, right up on the apex of a hill, two small figures between two gates in the fences, where I suppose there was some slight barrier to baffle the wind. The water was pouring off the fields in a sheet, and the road was a river in places. My hat, mac, and wellies were useless, and in no time I was soaked to the skin. But I got to them, and they looked in a sad way, especially Topper. Their heads hung down and they seemed lifeless.

A handful of damp pony nuts from my pocket brought a spark of lift to each, and I managed to hook a bridle over Topper and urge him on. Ned followed, and their feet squelched along in a spiritless plod. They had got so cold.

"Well done!" their owner cried when I got them back on to the road. I think she meant it - end I felt like a prefect praised by the head girl!

We brought them back together, and it was good to see them turn into their own stable at last, even though they had no straw under-foot. At least they were out of the terrible gale, against which I had fought my way bent double. A hot bath and change of clothes soon revived me, and they were none the worse for their ordeal.

*Feeding Ned and Topper*

When they were separated, after years together, I had the wretched job of seeing Topper into the horse box as the owner was called away. A relative of the family was going to have him, where he would have another pony for company and, I think, a good home. Ned's future was unknown at that stage. The horse box was luxurious and the young man who came for Topper was gentle and kind; he was used to transporting racehorses. The task was accomplished with relative ease, but I hated it, and when the horse box left, I shut myself in an empty stable and had a good howl. Then I went and bought pounds of carrots for Ned to console him.

He took the separation better than I expected. He went up and down the two fields whinnying off and on, but I went and got Katie, the goat, back (more of this anon), and they soon became better friends than they had previously been. Nobody knew what was to become of Ned, but within a fortnight he was offered to me, and the new owners of the fields gladly offered him permanent residence, with stabling in the winter, so his little story has, I hope, come to the "lived happily ever after" stage.

Just before Topper went, I enquired what was to become of Kelly. I had been looking after her, putting her in and out each day, for two years, and latterly supplying her goat food. Her owner "didn't quite know what to do with her."

My spadework was done already, so I was able to say that Paul liked her and would be glad to give her a home, as he had a paddock and stable available.

"Oh, well, he can have her," came the reply.

How casually some people dispose of their animals.

So, early one morning (before minds could be changed), Kelly and I marched through the village, across the bridge, along the lane, through the field, and into her new stable. I left her looking over the half-door in dismay. At lunch time I went to see her and let her out into the paddock to sample the grass. Kelly glued herself to me and wouldn't eat a mouthful, so after a while I put her back in the stable. In the evening I took her out again and the same thing happened.

After about three days of thrice daily visits she began to munch here and there, always keeping a sharp eye on me. I sat on the bank with a crossword book, but three hours out of each busy day was quite a chunk. When I wasn't with her, she gazed over her half door with her ears drooping, calling miserably. Kelly did not approve of her new home at all.

When Topper left, I went and fetched her back to her old home, which was gladly offered, and I was happy that now she and Ned would have each other for company.

"Come on," I told her, "you're going home, old dear."

I'm sure she knew it. I didn't put on her tether until we got to the road and she trotted briskly along beside me, occasionally pausing to stand on her hind legs and pick a tasty piece of bramble from the hedge. When Kelly does this, she is much taller than I am. When she wishes to run, I have to run with her if she is being led, as she is too strong for me to hold her back, and when the pace gets too swift - and she can run fast - I have to let go, unless I wish to travel at the horizontal.

*Taking the goat for a walk*

She behaved well through the village that day, and I was proud of her, especially as technically she too was now mine at last. We stopped at the door of one house, where a friend was looking out of the window in amusement; Kelly knew what was in the offing, and stood there patiently waiting for the biscuit which was soon offered.

She and Ned are now usually together, and the occasional chase he gives her is more mischief than anything. The two figures, one brown and the other off-white, bring life to the fields, and so do I on the odd occasions when she won't come in and I have to catch her. This is usually when some sheep have got in and she wants to stay with them, but it can also be when she gets That Certain Feeling several times a year, and is preoccupied, calling for a billy-goat.

Sometimes she gets out through the fence, and I have to go in search of her, and I know that I shall always find her with the sheep. She got rounded up with a flock once and was marked with a red blob on her flank. The farmer's five-year-old son, who did it, chortled gleefully, "Now us'll know the bugger."

When I went to catch her, I have to lure her with biscuits, and usually get her without too much difficulty, resentment, and tossing of horns. Her former owner once went in search of two corks to put on the end of these, but I haven't had to resort to such measures yet.

Goats' eyes are odd. The black pupil isn't round but a thin bar, which crosses the eye from east to west.

These are my special animals, but there are others for which I feel concern. The Exmoor farmer, from what I have seen, isn't over-careful of his sheep. Some of them, Eva once said to me, "are wicked!" I've seen many a half-starved one, its fleece hanging in tatters, scratching a meagre living for itself in the winter. I've also rescued quite a few which have caught themselves in the brambles or barbed wire and struggled until their fleece has twisted into a thick rope, from which they would never get free in their weakened states.

A sharp-edged stone is the tool to look for, so that one can saw through the rope while talking quietly to the frightened animal. Once on their feet, they are all right. But I wish more farmers would walk their land and see to their flocks properly, instead of keeping too many on the moor for the sake of the subsidies.

I once went and fetched a farmer acquaintance to see to one of his sheep, which was on the side of the road and obviously in distress.

"Ar," he said. "Us'll take un back down 'ome."

He opened my car door, which I held for him, and in no time the sheep was lying on the back seat. It was a new car. And it had cloth seats!

The autumn mornings cause me sad and angry feelings, because now the hunting starts up again, and it is deeply entrenched in North Devon. Stag and fox hounds meet three times a week, and earlier on the foxhounds are taken after the cubs. There are other vile practices too, when hares and rabbits are the quarry of beagle packs, and now there are mink hounds as well.

I make no secret of my views on hunting. I think it cruel to the animal and degrading to the participants, and a lot of what happens is carefully concealed from the public.

A master of the foxhounds has twice been to see me in response to my letters, signed by half a dozen of us, asking that hounds be kept out of the village, for the sake of all our domestic pets. Nothing doing - you come up against a kind of supercilious arrogance. These people delight to look down on others as "townies", if they are critical of hunting, but in my case I was able to say smartly that I'd had the cottage for nearly twenty years, and could introduce him to people country-born and bred who were equally opposed to it, including one ex-huntsman who gave up because he was sickened by the cruelty of it.

Last year I saw a fox running across the field just up the hill from my garden, some moments in advance of the hounds. I hope he got away... he looked so little and so alone.

There are times when animal populations have to be controlled, sometimes for their own good, but every living creature is entitled to humane treatment at the hand of man. They are our responsibility, not here to be abused. Deer can be culled by high-powered rifles with telescopic sights, using skilled marksmen. There is no need to hound them to exhaustion before shooting them. We often hear the argument that without hunting, in which the farmers can join, they would shoot the deer to extinction. My answer is that the deer, like all wildlife, belong to all of us and I am a firm advocate of properly administered management scheme with some compensation for farmers whose land and crops are raided by deer. If we can send men to the moon, and bring them back to a designated spot on earth, surely few problems are beyond the wit of man to solve, and this goes for the animal problems too.

Happily, more people are speaking out against the outdated and barbaric cruelties of hunting nowadays, and things are slowly getting better for the animals, especially as there are more questions being asked in parliament about these matters.

The razzamatazz of the red coats and hounds and horses could still be enjoyed if draghunting were to be encouraged. Here, a trail is laid in advance of the hounds, and I have been told by an official of the League against Cruel Sports that where practiced, draghunts are so popular that they are never advertised.

Exmoor's wild animals have given me many exciting and happy moments. I shall never forget standing in a lonely combe, with the sun setting in a red ball behind me, watching stags, hinds, and calves streaming up the opposite slope, their coats turned russet-red in the sunset.

Shy badgers are hard to see, but I have glimpsed them rustling away about their business, along their secret pathways in the bracken. I have watched hares on the moor, and enjoyed the beauty and grace of a fox who stopped to stare at me in the woods, before speeding away. I was amused by a stoat, once, who sat up in the heather to quiz me. Grey squirrels and rabbits are part of my morning walk with Patch, until the autumn days grow cold enough to send the squirrels into partial hibernation. I have watched mink in the riverbank, and other small creatures who dive away before I can be sure what they are. There is no such thing as a dull walk.

In the garden I am always pleased to see a toad or a hedgehog, and am careful not to disturb any piles of leaves in a corner, which, look as if they have been put there, in case I have a guest for the winter.

How much they give us, and how little they ask, all the creatures who share this world with us. These words from St. Francis of Assisi sum up my feelings exactly. "Not to hurt our humble brethren is our first duty to them, but to stop there is not enough. We have a higher mission - to be of service to them whenever they require it."

# Purple And Gold

Like a proud king-emperor, Exmoor loves to wear the royal colours of purple and gold. Sometimes these flicker along the hedge-rows in bright ribbons, and sometimes they flame across moor and hillside with all the drama of a flamboyant cloak.

My walk in the mornings takes me alongside a sunny, sheltered bank, and here, as early as February, I can see the first bright gold of the year. Celandines positively glitter in the sun, and I always feel guilty when I stop to admire them, for it can be a most invasive plant, and in my garden I pull them up. Even a tiny bulbil, artfully breaking off, will quickly start another plant - and off it goes again. It is related to the buttercup and its leaves remind me of watercress. If it was rare, we should probably fight to get it, for it has many virtues; it flowers early and generously; the flowers are beautiful; it has vanished neatly away by early summer. But it is too much of a good thing in a garden, and its place is among wild treasures.

Next, the palest and loveliest of flowers, comes the primrose. I can look out of the window by my desk and see the top of a field thick with them in April. A careful walk amongst them shows several interesting variations... double ones, odd polyurethane-like ones, and some which haven't made up their minds whether or not to be half-cowslip. These do make lovely garden plants and I encourage them, but I think they always look their best as nature meant them to grow. They have an innocent air, when their wide faces gaze up at the sun, and they smell of good white bread and butter, as these used to smell when bread was properly baked and not steam-baked, and butter could be had from a farmer's wife.

Just across the road, over the river, daffodils have naturalized themselves and gild the bank -perhaps from garden bulbs thrown into the water and washed up to gain a foothold. I notice that the sheep don't eat them, or the slugs either. Alas, even the daffodils which. I grow in tubs fall victim to champing jaws, and can end up frayed to bits. Oh, why do gardens have to have slugs?

In May, the gorse comes into its glory. Sheets of it light up the hillsides, and when the sun shines it dazzles the eyes. In September, a shorter variety – Western gorse – mixes with the mauve heather and purple bell heather and makes an unforgettable combination. Have you noticed that gorse smells of coconut?

Gold, of course, is the very colour of autumn. The larch wood opposite the cottage turns a beautiful soft yellowy-gold, and against it the shoulder of the hill is rich with amber bracken. Dave always calls it his "golden hill." The birches shower down their sovereigns, and last of all, the oaks change colour. Their yellow ochre slowly deepens to brown, and the leaves cling long, so that one can use them for winter vases.

Exmoor's purple, in all its tints, tends to be highly dramatic. A hillside flaming with early summer rhododendrons is a breath-taking sight. I have seen a sheet of pinky-mauve covering the side of a steep combe, and elsewhere pouring down a headland almost to the sea. It is not native to Britain, but since its introduction it has naturalized, and it spreads rapidly. There are locals here who can point to a hill covered with it which, in their childhood, was open pasture.

Red campions have woven skeins of a similar colour along the hedgerows just before the foxgloves arrive in their hundreds. Their green steeples slowly open buds which are tinged with pink, and then deepen to purple, spotted within, and raided by the bumblebees. The spots are their runway markers, guiding them in to the hidden nectar. They go in so neatly, and then clamber out' awkwardly back-wards, and if you gently pinch the lips of the flower together so that the bee can't get out for a moment she buzzes very angrily indeed.

Dave's golden hill has a great moment in mid-summer, when it is covered with rosebay willowherb. What a beautiful plant this is; glorious, glowing cerise, and worthy of a place in the garden, were it not like the celandine – too much of a good thing. In September you can see its seeds floating off on wisps of down with every passing breeze.

Just up the valley is a steep stony slope, almost scree, where the bell heather is a sizzling magenta in summer. When it meets a sky of Exmoor blue above, the colours shout. Nobody would wear such contrasts, but nature gets away with it every time.

And last of all, in one great, magnificent finale, the heather or ling, comes out. A pink smoke begins to drift over the moors in August, deepening slowly to rich purple, and the scent comes sweetly on the air. In September, as you walk through it, clouds of pollen dust your feet, and the bees are delirious.

Heather honey is much sought-after, but it is the devil to extract and needs special equipment. It is dark, and has a jelly-like consistency in the comb. I would rather my bees didn't fly that far, but they do – three miles is about their limit. Heather has had many uses in the past apart from its contribution to honey making. It has been used as thatch, bedding, fuel, and even basketry material. It gives an orange dye, and dries quite well for winter flower arrangements, retaining its colour and a faint tang of the moors.

As autumn draws on, the purple slowly turns to brown, and the show is over for another year. The swallows leave as the heather fades, and there is a sense of things quietening down of glad rags folded away, because the party's over, and the pageant has passed.

# The Bees And The Birds

I became a beekeeper at midday while I was at work. A colleague's brother-in-law was a keen beekeeper, and his name was on a list used by the police when stray swarms were reported and had to be removed. I made it known that I was keen to have bees, and was already in possession of a hive. The grape vine worked, and hence the phone call which I received at work. A small swarm was available for me.

I arranged to collect the bees in their travelling accommodation on a Friday evening, and drove straight down to Devon with them. Valerie, who was already "into" bees was waiting excitedly to greet me. We lifted the box containing the bees onto the base of my hive, and left them closed in for the night. The next morning we put them into the hive proper, the entrance was unblocked, and I sat myself down nearby to watch my very own bees come out of my very own hive. This, I felt, was the real stuff of country life.

At first, they are just bees going in and out. Then you start to notice differences. Some are bigger than others. Some have little bags on their back legs which are in different colours – brown, yellow, orange, mauve. You ask yourself what they are doing, for there is a definite air of purpose about their activity. Some of them fly off (Will they come back?), and some walk about on the little platform at the hive entrance. Two of them appear to be having a wash and brush up. Horrors – a dead one is being poked out of the hive! Why? What? How?

I suddenly realised that I knew nothing at all about bees and beekeeping beyond what I had gleaned from some very sketchy reading and some interesting conversations with one of two people. I set out to learn. I borrowed books from the library, but they all seemed too advanced, and some made rather heavy reading. I rang up the colleague's brother-in-law so frequently with my anxious questions that I'm sure he was on the point of saying to his wife, "If it's her again, I'm out!" One old country chap told me, "There aint nothing much to keeping bees." Valerie knew quite a bit, but I wanted to be independent.

I decided to enroll myself on a beginners" course for bee-keeping, and hoped that my bees would take care of themselves meanwhile. After all, there had been a neglected hive in the garden of Valerie's house for seven years before she brought it, and they had survived without human assistance until her arrival.

The course was very basic and dealt with such simple things as the names of the various parts of the hive and its equipment. I knew a little more than this, so I gained a bit of confidence. Then, of course, one came up against the "star pupil", who had read all the books, kept bees, and asked all the interesting questions, conducting a kind of advanced mini-course with the tutor. The rest of us exchanged looks, and confided our lack of know-how to each other. I took copious notes, and was unintentionally responsible for giving the class a good laugh before we finished the course.

Our tutor was dealing with feeding the bees in the autumn, and gave us the recipe for making the syrup. This was 10lbs. of white sugar to 5 pints of water, heated until the sugar dissolved.

"Any questions, anybody?" she concluded.

I put up my hand. "wouldn't it be better for the bees if it was made with brown sugar?"

"No," she replied. "They aren't health food addicts."

Valerie supervised my bee-feeding that first autumn, and all was quiet until the spring when the bees got busy again as the days warmed up. Then I felt my lack of knowledge to be a real handicap. One must, said the books, open the hive on a nice warm day in

April and look through it. Look through it for what? One should check the brood. If the spring was late and cold, one should decide whether or not to feed again. And later, one should watch out for queen cells and prepare for swarm control.

I donned all my gear, lit my smoker and took the roof off the hive? Then I started to lift out the frames, all covered in bees, and looked at each one. Then I put them back. I was none the wiser...but I had "looked through them" all on my own, which made me feel good, but at the same time underlined my ignorance.

By this time, Valerie had met a dear old boy who lived for his bees, and he was helping her, but soon the position was reversed as his strength and health began to fail. I became the willing assistant at times, and my stock of knowledge began to grow. I would watch with interest to see a new-born bee wriggle free from its brood cell, and I became quite good at spotting the queen on a frame of bees from the brood chamber. She slipped out of sight as quickly as she could, seeming almost shy and humble, although she is the center of the hive's life and purpose, and without her the bees are doomed.

I could now identify and talk knowingly about brace comb, drone cells, queen cells, pollen sacs, and the like, and I would handle frames of bees with confidence. I needed a lesson, and I got one.

Going to put a container of food on my hive, one autumn afternoon, I thought that it wasn't necessary to light my smoker and put on my white beekeeper's suit and veiled hat and gloves. I'll only be a minute, I thought. Then I accidentally humped the hive, and out they all came. Bees are naturally vigilant to protect their food store in the autumn, and they can quickly get angry if they think there's an intruder. I was lucky that the garden shed was close by, into which I fled, and I got away with seven stings on my head and face, and a few on my hands.

There was a character called Miss Piggy in a childrens' T.V programme who had little slit eyes above bulging cheeks. That was who was looking at me from my dressing table mirror the next morning! However, the swellings went down after 24hours, and the irritation subsided, and I duly recorded a lesson learnt.

One day, while I was at work, I got a 'phone call from a neighbor in Devon, saying that my bees had swarmed, but not to worry, as the nice old boy whom Valerie knew had been contacted and he had taken the swarm. It now resided in a box in my garden.

I felt rather guilty, as I know a lot of people are wary, if not scared, of bees, and the tutor on my beginners' course had warned us that anyone within half a mile of your hive who gets stung will always say it is one of your bees. Would there be a queue of irate villagers awaiting me at the weekend?

It wasn't too bad. One neighbour said that there had been bees everywhere, and the wife of the then landlord of the pub called to express her concern in case any of the guests in the hotel-part got stung. I thought that it would be kind and considerate if I moved my hive, until I could be there all the time to look after things, and I was delighted when the rector of a nearby church offered to have the hive in the rectory garden. He had always kept bees himself, and missed them, and I was glad to have another source of experience to tap.

I borrowed a spare base from Valerie, and transferred the bees which were left in the hive onto it, making a mini colony, for the time being. Then I took all the rest of the equipment up to the rectory, and set up the hive again. The next morning came the nerve-racking part. I had wrapped the box containing the swarm in a sheet, before the bees began to fly, in the early morning. This I lifted into another cardboard box, for safety's sake, and transferred the lot to the boot of a friend's car, as it was too big to go in mine. He drove, and I sat leaning over the boot, steadying the box. It was only a ten-minute journey, taken at a steady pace so as not to rock the bees.

Casually my friend asked how many bees were in the box.

"It's quite a big swarm," I replied. "There could be 3O,OOO or more."

He accelerated considerably after that.

Hiving a swarm is an interesting and somehow touching experience. You arrange a white cloth from the ground in front of the hive up to its entrance, smoothing it out into a nice wrinkle-free surface. Then you take whatever contains the swarm and jerk them all out on to the cloth. They spread out and mill about for a bit, and then they begin to move in a great army up the cloth and into the hive. They are taking possession of their new home, and somewhere in their midst is their most precious possession – their queen. You hang over them, trying to spot her, and you marvel at the organisation which has led these tiny creatures forth in search of more spacious accommodation. The old hive has been left stocked with queen cells, from one of which will emerge a new young queen, who will go round and kill all the other queens as they came out, and thus make herself "Queen Bee". It is the old queen who has led out the swarm, and she will now be frantic to start laying her eggs to ensure the continuity of the colony.

It is surprising how many phrases in our language relate to bees and hives, indicating how common beekeeping once was – before the importation of sugar, I suppose. A hive of industry; as sweet as honey; as busy as bees; swarms of people; she's the Queen Bee; a bit of a drone; a sting in the tail.... No wonder that conical straw skeps often appear in old illustrations, and even in stained glass windows and carvings on pew ends in churches.

I presently took the remaining colony from my garden up to the rectory, and there the two hives stayed for two or three years.

The rector helped and advised me, and my knowledge and experience grew.

Eventually one lot swarmed. As always, they first clustered close to the hive, but before I could get up there to collect the swarm, the bees had taken off and we never found them. The rector was most upset, and spent quite a few hours walking the hedgerows looking for them. We asked the nearest people to let us know if bees arrive in their barns or lofts or stables, but nothing was heard from any-one, so we assumed that somewhere they had found a hollow tree or a hole in a bank or wall which suited them, and settled there.

I was walking along a track on the moor once when I got a strong smell of honey. Looking down, I saw a few dead bees by a scraped-out hole. Had a fox found a colony in a rabbit hole, and dug it out for the sweet harvest?

I was not dismayed at losing a swarm, because I really only wanted one hive, to give me a little honey for my own use each year. Valerie said that in that case we could now take the bees from which the lost swarm came, remove the queen cells, and unite the two hives. This we did successfully, and I was pleased to be back to one hive again.

I shared my honey with the rector, and here I must say that never will there be a sweeter taste than that of my very first honey. I had an extractor, a gadget like a milk churn into which the frames are fixed, after the wax cappings have been sliced off. You then turn the handle and the frames spin round, throwing the honey out by centrifugal force. After all this laborious and sticky process, there it was....a fragrant golden bounty, made after countless visits to the flowers by my bees. The time was half-past two, and I cut some bread and butter, boiled the kettle, and sat down to my tea there and then. A moment never to be forgotten!

Both the rector and Valerie agreed that it was very good honey

Indeed.

A change of incumbent, alas, meant that all too soon my kind friend moved on, and as his successor was not bee-minded. I accepted Valerie's offer of a spot in her paddock. My bees hadn't been able to go there on their first move because it was too close to the cottage. Unless they are dormant, in the middle of winter you can only move them "three feet or three miles", as the saying is. Back to the village they came, and we put them at the end of the row where Valerie had her six hives.

That year I was able to help her quite a bit. It was a bad year for swarming, and with all her stock she had a lot of swarms. It was nice to be able to help and repay some of her kindness, especially as her husband was not keen on bees.

"He gave me a hand once," she explained graphically, "but the

bees got angry and the last I saw of Don was when he disappeared down the garden path, doing a sort of tribal dance and shouting, "Bloody bees! Bloody bees?"

The most memorable help I gave her was when a prime swarm clustered in the branches of a willow tree on the edge of her paddock. She had got a step ladder wedged against the trunk, and had fixed a home-made skep just above the swarm, and the bees had gone up into it. The problem now was how to get the skep safely down with the bees inside it. We decided that if I held a board on my head, she could lower the skep onto it and thus the swarm would be secured and could be hived before the bees took off again.

The step ladder wobbled, and I had to stand balanced with one leg in the ditch, clutching the square of board on my head with both hands. Every other phrase from the tree seemed to be, "Hang on." Then came the triumphant cry, "I've got it!"

With great care Valerie came down a couple of steps on the ladder clasping the skep, and a prime swarm is no light weight. There was then a bump as she got it onto my waiting board, and there I stood crowned with at least 50,000 bees. And what did I do? No, I didn't slip and let the whole lot so, but I started to laugh. So did she.

"Why-are-you-laughing?" she got out.

"I-don't-know. Its-so-ridiculous!"

What-is?"

"Standing-here-with-all-these-bees-on-my-head!"

We calmed down shortly, and lowered the board so that we could carry it between us to the empty hive awaiting the swarm. There, having been shaken out onto a piece of white sheet, the slow march of the bees into their new home began, and we stood and watched, hot and disheveled, but full of satisfaction at a job successfully concluded.

Not long afterwards, Valerie and her husband moved on. Things hadn't worked out for them as happily as expected. And I think they were wise to go. We've lost touch now, as they've had yet got another move; things were never the same after the lost kitten episode (now my Sammie), but I remember the good times.

I managed my bees on my own then. The new owner of the house was quite happy for me to keep the hive on his land, but asked if I could move it to the other side of the hedge and further from the house, which I did in the middle of the winter. They now had a nice, sheltered corner close to the river, and here it was that the following autumn I had my most unnerving experience with bees.

It concerned feeding them, again. I'd had one lesson, but foolishly I took another chance. I had extracted my honey and had super full of frames which I wished to put back in the hive for the bees to clean. (A super is a Kind of square box with no top or bottom, in which the frames of comb are suspended. When you have extracted the honey from these, the bees will clear out what is left and take it down into their winter store.) It would only take me a couple of minutes to lift off the roof and a part of the outer hive, put on a super, replace the pieces, and go.

I had my veiled hat on, and my smoker was lit, but I didn't wear my white suit. I had on a red sweater, and it was rather a windy day. Bees don't like wind, it makes them touchy. They don't like bright colours, either. I knew this, in theory. Now I was to learn for real! I took the roof off, and the crown board, which is the lid that keeps the bees in. I removed the outer part and lowered the super onto the hive. And out they poured, very angry indeed at the interference. Then my smoker went out, so I had nothing to control them with.

In no time at all I had a brown mat of bees all over my front and arms, and the stings were going in one after the other. For one wild moment I thought I might have to jump in the river to get them off, but having fled some distance from the hive, beating them off as I ran, I got them clear, and made for home. Within minutes the irritation started, and before ten had passed I was dancing on the spot, itching even on the soles of my feet and scratching like a mad thing.

I had to get someone to drive me to the local cottage hospital, where the nurse asked, while I waited for the doctor, where "the" bee had stung me.

I must have got upwards of fifty stings, but magically, one jab stopped the torment, and I was sent home with some tablets to take, sore from scratching, but otherwise none the worse. But that time I did learn my lesson. And now I never take chances, and I treat my bees with respect, and dress accordingly, with due regard to the season and the weather conditions.

I had fled, that autumn afternoon, without putting the roof back on, and in the evening it began to rain lightly, so I waited until dark and then, clad in my gear, I went and made all to rights holding my breath, I think.

I must confess that I was, for a time, less enthusiastic about beekeeping, but I was reluctant to give my hive away. Then I met another beekeeper from not far away. He had eight hives and loved his bees, and was only too pleased to share his skill and knowledge. Together we have sorted out a few problems in my hive, and I have helped him to transport some of his. We nearly had fun and games with his last hive, as the bees found a way out and were emerging into the car – fortunately just as we arrived at his apiary.

I look forward to many pleasant bee sessions in future. My confidence has come back, and with it the wonder at the marvelous activity and organisation of these industrious little creatures. As someone once said, "They are more civilized than we are, really, because they are all working for each other and not just for themselves."

And now for the birds.

Birds are an important part of my life at the cottage. They flock to the bird table I made for them, and sometimes there are so many tits clustering on and around the nut container that it looks like a bunch of blue grapes. Truly! The comings and goings of all of them keep the garden alive on even the darkest days, and the colder it gets the more they crowd in. The tits are fewer in summer, but when the swallows leave in the autumn, they return in a lively crowd and keep me constantly amused with their antics.

I used to hang the nuts further down the garden, but a hawk, attracted by all the fluttering, came flashing down on three occasions and picked off a blue tit, so I made a roofed bird table and sited it closer to the house, which foiled him. I have just made a bigger one, and moved it even closer, so now I can watch them a few feet from the kitchen window. Close-by is an old tractor wheel disc, set into the ground, a find on the moor, which makes an excellent bird bath and drinking place for them.

My first job every morning is to clean the bird table, top up the nuts, fill the seed dish, and put bread and other scraps in readiness for the first arrivals. Robbie, my tame robin, usually flutters round for her first breakfast crumbs, which she eats from my hand, then the tits arrive – blue, great, and cole tits, – and after them the sparrows and chaffinches. I have two blue tits which will take bits of biscuit from my hand, and the thrill of feeling those cold, tiny claws clutching round my finger is indescribable. I feel so humble to be honored like this by creatures which are so truly wild and free.

The tits have to be waited for patiently, but Robbie follows me about, even outside the garden, and I talk to her constantly. When I call her, she darts up the garden, and sometimes if I'm busy she will attract my attention by fluttering round my head, or flying straight at me with a last minute swoop to one side. I love Robbie dearly, and study her feather arrangements and beak and claws closely when she is pecking up her crumbs. These have to be biscuit or cake; I offered her breadcrumbs once, and my fingers got a series of sharp peeks of disapproval. It was quite unmistakable.

I read somewhere that robins are not long-lived, about two years is their life expectancy, so Robbie is especially dear. Those bright brown and black eyes look up at me without fear, and although a bird has no facial expressions, the attitude tells the mood of the moment. Robbie will lean forward to peer, full of curiosity; her head will show a little crest of raised feathers when she wishes to warn off another bird; if I'm not quick enough with her crumbs she will impatiently fly at my hand, dab it with her feet, and land on a near-by twig for attention; things can make her jump, literally, when she will shoot up into the air for a few inches, all of a fluttery dither. Given half a chance, she will hop through the conservatory and arrive on the kitchen table, being nosey, and even help herself from a bowl of cereal, but I don't' encourage this. If Sammie were to appear, there could be a tragedy.

The blue tits also come into the conservatory if I leave the door open for long. I started to scatter a few crumbs on the table for them, but then thought better of it for the same reason.

This is an area rich in bird life. My bird table visitors include the three varieties of tits mentioned, sparrows, chaffinches, greenfinches, a wren, and occasionally a siskin; blackbirds and thrushes ground feed in the colder weather, when the starlings also appear. A pair of jays has visited, and a magpie. A spotted woodpecker came for about three weeks to the nut containers.

At night I hear owls calling from the wood over the river. On my walks, I see at various times long-tailed tits, dippers, grey and yellow wagtails as well as the pied ones, herons, goldfinches, yellow hammers, redstarts, wheatears, jackdaws, rooks, crows, ravens, the cuckoo, buzzards, skylarks, treecreepers, fieldfares, redwings bramblings, hawks, curlew, lapwings, grouse, pheasants, and, of course, house martins, swifts and swallows.

On the seashore, there are various gulls, cormorants, and sandpipers, and once I think I glimpsed a puffin. There are mallards on the river together with other ducks, variety unknown, and a kingfisher has recently been seen along the river near the cottage, but not as yet by me. There are also all those little brown birds, which slip away into the hedges and defy identification, although sometimes, as with the migrant chiffchaff, their song gives the clue. And all these birds – and I'll have surely left some out of the list – have been seen casually in passing, so a real bird watcher would add many more.

We all got excited in the village one autumn by glimpses of a most beautiful little bird, whose wings and body flashed with a soft, glowing scarlet. Books were consulted, and theories were expounded. Then Phil, our local semi-retired clergyman, managed to get a photograph as it visited his bird table. Clearly, our Red Bird was an aviary escapee, and soon it disappeared, and our excitement died down. We were not about to make the national press with a rare continental visitor.

People sometimes enquire as to the whereabouts of the peregrine falcon, which I have seen once or twice (and I left him off my list) but on the whole, the less common the bird the better is a policy of vagueness. Look how the ospreys in Scotland have to be guarded.

Some of us are naughty enough to wish that the peacocks at the guest house would "disappear", especially at mating time. Their raucous banshee cries do not blend with the local birds, and at three o'clock in the morning they drive guests at the hotel mad when they fly up on to the roof and let forth. Shoes have been flung out of windows, and dogs have been urged to give chase, but these wretched birds just hoot and shriek and fly off into someone's garden. I have shrieked, too, as their floundering tails drag across my seed bed! Then one catches sight of one of the males, strutting with his tail fanned out in all its glory in the sun, and somehow all is forgiven at such an outstanding example of nature's bravado.

My cockerel, Harold, has also incurred disfavor by his early morning fanfares, but at least his don't come from just over a bedroom window.

Harold and his hen-ladies have had a chequered career. He belonged to the guest house, and got left behind when the previous owners vacated, and it was awaiting sale. Then the pub took them on, and Harold and his ladies were confined to a stable. This was right underneath the flat where the landlord and his wife lived, so Harold's dawn crowings were not popular at all. Foreseeing trouble, I offered to make them a hen house and run in a corner of the field. This done, I transferred them to it, but unfortunately the horses, Topper and Ned, soon got the smell of the hens' food, and kept breaking down the wire netting to get at it.

Almost every day, I would go out to shut Harold and his ladies in for the night, and find that they had all got out and gone back to the guest house. I would round them up and shepherd them to their new address, Harold grumbling all the way. Sometimes one of the hens would flap off towards the wood, and I would give chase, which caused the others much distress, cluckings and crowings. These performances took up nearly an hour every night, and in the end I asked if I could have them for my own and put them in my garden.

Their egg-laying was a bit spasmodic and the novelty had long worn off, so Harold and co.., were mine. I dismantled and moved their house and transferred them in a packing case to another new home. Here they lived for two or three years. Age took its toll, and Harold's harem was reduced to two from the original six. Then the pub changed hands. The new owners had three dogs, one of which became obsessed with the hens. He prowled and blew and barked up and down the fence which made one side of their run, and eventually wriggled in. It was all a great game for him, and the two hens broke loose, leaving poor old Harold in solitary distress.

After half a day's searching, we found and got them both back, but we were all worried about their future, in spite of the new wire netting which was fixed all along the boundary fence for me.

Then these kind people offered me the old greenhouse enclosure which adjoins my garden. This has a wall round it, with pig wire on top, and with very little effort it was converted into a deluxe run for Harold and his ladies. I moved his house yet again, and here they settled, three O.A.P's. relaxing in their declining years. Bags of bread and greens appeared regularly from the hotel for my little flock and, another problem solved!

Once or twice I have forgotten to shut the hen house up for the night, and, in the way of such things, I haven't remembered until I was in bed. On such occasions a strange sight could have been seen in my garden. A figure with a torch flitting down the garden path, clad in a long nightdress, a duffel coat, and a pair of wellington boots. Clutching an umbrella, if wet.

# Harvest Festival

All the little churches that I know, scattered about North Devon, continue the ancient and beautiful tradition of harvest festival. One famous church, where the winter congregation can number just five, bulges at the seams and every pew is crammed for the occasion, and heads must be ducked to avoid the mass of greenery spilling from the windowsills.

One enters through a porch, where pots and jars of flowers hint at the beauty within. Just inside the door, the font is surrounded with branches of beech and oak in their rich autumn colours, and on the top, all the late glories of the garden thrust forth from a great colorful bowl. The lectern is wreathed with corn dollies, and the pulpit is hazardous for the rector, because one of the "flower ladies" has excelled herself in a sweeping arrangement of leaves, flowers and berries, which is balanced on the windowsill behind.

("And now to God the Father..."he says, removing a rowan: berry from his left ear.)

In front of the old choir stalls – empty nowadays, except for today, when late-comers have to sit there bashfully, in full view of the rest – there are more swags of golden beech. The altar is dressed with greenery and fruit, and has a centerpiece of the traditional bread-wheatsheaf, made by a local baker. Clean-washed vegetables spill from the chancel steps and windowsills, and the rich smell of apples and pears mingles with the sharp tang of Chrysanthemums and the sweet scent of late roses.

Farmers who never come to church in the ordinary way appear for harvest festival, their burly Devon voices hammering out the old hymns; "Fair waved the golden corn"; "Now thank we all our God"; "We plough the fields and scatter". For once, the lady-organist is nearly out-done.

There is something timeless about the festival in this tiny church. Like a little flame, its light has flickered the message of Christianity across the fields and along the valley since pre-Saxon times. Its path is worn and the steps are hollowed by the passage of feet over long, long years. To the sophisticated, harvest festival may be a quaint survival from years gone by. But I wonder. We might all be the better for a simple faith, like the kind that can sing out;

*"He only is the maker*

*Of all things near and far;*

*He paints the wayside flower,*

*He lights the evening star;*

*The winds and waves obey Him,*

*By Him the birds are fed;*

*Much more to us, His children,*

*He gives-our daily bread."*

Look at the order and pattern and organisation on which the whole universe is founded. Can one doubt that underlying it is Intelligence of a supreme and unimaginable nature?

There are strawberries and raspberries in the freezer, and in store are enough potatoes – Foremost, Pentland Ivory and King Edward – to last me until the new ones come again. Two net bags of onions hang in the conservatory, along with a couple of pounds of shallots and some garlic.

In the garden there are lettuce under lemonade bottles, and first early onions showing green shoots. Good Spinach is ready for picking and, under its corrugated plastic tunnel, will give me a harvest till the spring. The sprouts are coming on well, so are the January King cabbages, and there are leeks tucked in all over the place.

My plans for next year are already devised. Harold's old run, forked over roughly, will grow maincrop potatoes. A new strawberry bed is planted with sturdy rooted runners. The site for cloched peas and beans, which I shall sow next month in pots, is ready. A huge compost heap is in the making. Extra garlic cloves have been planted as I love this health-giving herb and use it more and more.

Ned and Kelly now have three horses to stay with them for the winter, and they all go in at night in a clattering troop. (Ned thinks he has died and gone to Paradise!) I have taken on the routine task of letting them all out in the morning, and I enjoy walking round to do this in the cold, clean air. There have been no hard frosts as yet this autumn, only a few slight ones that crisped the fallen leaves and powdered them with a touch of white.

We put our clocks back at the end of October, and now the evenings are long and the fireside is welcoming. My wood store is packed with branches to be sawn up. I like to be up at first light, so as to hurry through my chores and get out into the garden for all the daylight hours possible. On wet days I can occupy myself for hours, clearing up – yet again– the untidy garden shed, and sorting out its contents. Sometimes I even thrown some of them away (but not very often. I am a hoarder.) Besides, they might "come in" for something.

At dusk, the heron flaps along the valley, his strange cry sounding for all the world, like someone scraping a garden spade clean. A dozen ducks come home in threes and fours to the lake which was made in a field up the valley some years ago. I linger outside, reluctant to go indoors, and wonder what sort of winter we shall get. Robbie comes for her last few crumbs, and I wonder where she goes to roost. Sometimes there will be a faint golden glow in the east, where a big moon is rising, while the sky in the west still wears its last fiery sunset glow.

I often stay in the garden until it is quite dark. I feel as if I am watching the season slowly slip away, until tomorrow it is November...and the start of my winter.

*Liz in the flower garden*

# Winter

"No flowers, no trees, no birds, no sun, November", my deputy used to chant gloomily at the start of that month. Once upon a time I would have agreed with him heartily, but not since I became a gardener. November now means the lighting up of the winter jasmine's yellow stars, and tulip-planting time. There is no better antidote to the gloom of a wet, dark November day than a browse along the garden center shelves in this section.

What romantic names they have! Queen of the Night, Apricot Beauty, Heart's Delight, Love Song, Dreaming Maid...and specialist catalogues read even better. I have tried lots of different ones, with varying results over the years. They all flower once, because bulbs are good nowadays. I plant them deeply, and leave them in when they've finished, and am not unduly dismayed if they don't come up again. If they did, my garden would be overcrowded...that is to say, more than it is already, and then I shouldn't have the pleasure of browsing and choosing all over again next year.

Queen of the Night was a great disappointment. She was so dark almost black, and she disappeared against her background, so I wasn't sorry when she abdicated. Shirley was elegant, in white and mauve, but wistful, and inclined to hide herself away amongst some nearby ferns. General de Wet, who should have flown brazen orange banners, sulked amongst his own leaves and lost his springtime battle. Apricot Beauty was a dream of delicate loveliness, as if a film star had strayed into my homely cottage garden, and I was sad that she never gave a repeat performance. She was quite expensive as well, a film star would be, wouldn't she- but I think I shall invite her to perform again next year. Parrot tulips I love, but find their great blowsy heads streaked with green are too heavy for their stems and they flop. One can't stake a tulip..., it would be like seeing the leading lady on a crutch, so I only have them occasionally. There are some new varieties which look unspeakably common, with stripes and ruffles and spikey bits all over them, and I wish that the breeders would attend to the flop instead of turning a quaint flower into a freak.

I have two faithful old friends, who do reappear for two or three years running. These are Beauty of Appeldoorn and Oxford. The first one is tall, with proud heads of a golden yellowy orange, which light up when the sun shines as if they hold a candle flame inside. Oxford is not quite so tall, and of a soft glowing red that never clashes with anything else. I plant more of each every year and welcome them with affection. Spring wouldn't be the same without them.

By the end of November the garden is tidied up for the winter, and the compost heap is piled high with ropes of old nasturtiums, broad bean and pea haulms, and beech hedge clippings. My potatoes are sorted, cleaned and stored, and the onions hang in net bags in the porch, along with a bunch or two of garlic. The lemonade bottles once again house little gem lettuce. The sprouts are staked against the gales. The winter cabbages no longer need daily inspection for eggs of caterpillars. All is neat and clean of weeds (usually), and there are fewer leaves to sweep up each day.

Last year, a mysterious pile of leaves appeared against the side of the conservatory. Strange little tapping noises could be heard at times from within it, and once or twice a small, hacking cough. One longed to investigate, and more, to do something about that cough, but one dare not interfere or else Hedgehog would leave. There he stayed, and once the winter cold bit, there were no more noises. I used to look at the pile and wonder if he was all right, but experience with wild life has taught me the golden rule DON'T

INTERFERE, unless some creature is obviously injured or sick and in need of help. Hedgehog was all right, and came out in the spring, and thereafter visited his corner every night to eat his supper inside the house that I made for him, to keep his food dry and out of reach of stray cats.

In the woods the winter gales strip the trees. The Little Prince

cast aside his golden crown long ago, and only the oaks retain their leaves. Leathery and brown, they make handsome winter dried arrangements with branches of larch cones and graceful, ghostly honesty.

When I take the woodland path with Patch, I look about for glossy ivy and its green berries, and holly, sparkling with red ones, and earmark my Christmas gathering. Not too much – just enough to fill a big pitcher, with a sprig for the Christmas pudd. The woods in winter can be so still and silent that the fall of a late acorn is startling, and the snapping of a twig sounds like a rifle shot,

There are jays about, and magpies, and most years a little flock of longtailed tits works up and down the valley, searching the small trees and bushes. Tulip-planting makes me think of spring, and although it is far, far away and too early to long for it, I am nevertheless glad to notice stubby catkins waiting on all the hazel trees.

The sounds of winter are fierce at times. The winds can roar through the valley like an express train, and the river in spate is equally noisy. On the beach, waves crash and suck at the shingle in stormy weather, and the high, wild keening of the gulls thrills me. What freedom is in that cry, what power in that flight as they hang quivering on the wind and then flash down to the water's level! Great gusts of air are flung into one's lungs until you and the elements seem one.

You can sometimes merge too much with the elements, as when slipping on a seaweedy rock and sitting down in the sea, or tramping through mud which pulls your boot right off and leaves you advancing with a foot in a soggy sock.

Silence too...the eerie one of fog, when the dank mists thicken and fill the valley, and the mournful wail of the foghorn comes from the point. Nobody drives out unless they have to, and only the odd land rover creeps through the village, raising hopes that, after all, we shall get a daily paper thanks to its driver. There comes, too, another kind of silence in December or January, which is more a kind of brooding hush as the grey clouds thicken and descend with menace in the murky air. The birds fall silent, slipping away to safe shelter before the snow.

It comes in little wet spits at first, then faster, in flakes that drive straight at you on a rising wind. The corner of the road is no longer visible and soon there are webs of white on the window where the snow has pitched. The road becomes level with the front doorstep and the steps in the garden disappear. Still that silence, broken only by a sighing of white, laden air.

We are all out with our spades the next day, when the snow has stopped, and the clanking music of our scraping combines with the cheerful shouts and comments as the news filters through.

"Main roads closed since last night."

"Road's blocked up the hill there's a delivery van turned over."

"'Tis bad over the moor"

"More to come, so the weatherman says."

"Ar," agrees Tam,

Certainly the sky looks full of it; the school bus can't get through, and soon high-pitched shouts are heard from the hill behind the village, as the home-made toboggans come out.

*The garden in winter*

Last winter the snow lay for a fortnight, and it was of that powdery kind which sticks to every twig. I got up early to scrape my doors clear, and then I was off with the dog to explore the winter wonderland. And what a wonderland! Everything was dressed in exquisite white lace, every tree and bush, every spike of old foxglove and bracken – all transformed into a radiance of white and diamonds. Nothing could be more beautiful and I walked two miles each morning before breakfast for three days running to marvel at it all. For contrast, the river was black as jet.

By the third day the tracks of animals and birds provided a new kind of book to read, and my neighbor's son and I went out across the fields to look.

There were the tiny marks of small creatures near the hedgerows, as they foraged, and all sorts of bird tracks from the hoppers and walkers. A fox had left his paw marks, scuffed in places by the drag of his brush. The rabbits appeared to have been playing, as their prints wove and twirled in dizzy circles all over the place. Where-as the fox seemed purposeful, trekking from the wood towards the farm, the rabbits suggested a carefree holiday attitude that, like the children, seized the fun inherent in this new, exciting situation.

I have been cut off here for three or four days, and had to get the police to contact "head office" on my behalf, there being no phone lines open. (This was much better than being marooned at the other end and unable to get here.) We then had the excitement of the helicopter arriving with bread, mail, and medicines sent by the local doctor for his regular patients. Modern equipment has ensured that before long a road will be opened, not like the old days when teams of men had to dig a way through, and the village once remained cut off for six weeks.

My late neighbor Den was quick to phone complaints if the snow plough was slow on the scene. This contraption works on a blower system, so that the snow is sucked in one way and then blown out again over the hedgerow, to right or left according to which way the blower is turned. I'm sure it was an accident when on one occasion the blower, shot a load through an open window and it all landed on Den's bed.

In the middle of winter, Christmas comes as a welcome interlude, when there is a kindly spirit abroad. We deliver our own cards to village cronies, and the flip of the letter box means that someone has surreptitiously slid one through and hastened off. It is not done to knock at the door and hand it over.

I hang my cards all-round the sitting room walls, and reserve those with robins on for the mantelpiece. These I keep from year to year, and I now have a large collection of robin cards for which I hope I shall one day find a use.

All along the mantelpiece are little branches of fir, which give off a spicey scent in the warmth. Glittering balls and tinsel twine in and out, and all the picture frames wear a crest of evergreen. When it is decorated for Christmas, I fall in love with my cottage all over again.

Usually I go to midnight mass on Christmas Eve, and this ancient festival overcomes all the false commercial trappings with its old peace and simplicity. Coming home afterwards, I stop in the dark to look down over the sea, and listen for the cry of the sheep from the surrounding hills. "And if it's true," I say with John Betjeman "and if it's true... it could have been just like this". The quiet night, the black velvet sky, the glittering stars, the sheep calling and suddenly, that terrifying, awesome splitting of the heavens and those unearthly voices. Two thousand years shrink away, and I could almost be there.

Already another marvel has occurred. Unsung, unnoticed, unremarked, the shortest day has come and gone. We have turned a stupendous cosmic corner, which only our forebears celebrated. No earthquakes or hurricanes thrust it upon our notice, but surely it has happened, and the year has turned towards light and warmth again.

There may yet be cold snaps and power cuts, when the knots in the string come undone and disrupt our local power supply. I shall then sleep downstairs by the fire with a good supply of logs and candles, rather than endure a bed that has no electric over-blanket.

"Nothing on earth," my deputy once said, "would induce me to go to bed knowing that I was connected to a power station." Nothing on earth will induce me to go to bed unconnected!

Snuggled up in the flickering firelight I dream of spring, happy in the knowledge that already the flower shops are selling daffodil buds, and by January will be full to overflowing with violets, jonquils, narcissi, and all the other early delights.

Winter isn't so bad after all! People

# Peoples

On one of my earliest visits to this part of the world, when I was barely twenty, I was taken to the village pub to be instructed in the art of shove ha'penny, and to meet some of the real locals.

These were the old farmers who could look back to the coming of the motor car to these narrow lanes, and for whom the second world war provided a nightly firework display. They would go up to the top road and look across to South Wales to see who was "getting it", watch the sky bloom as far away as Bristol.

Grandfather Sturge believed in comfort, even while on Home Guard duty. He took an armchair up to his check point.

Evacuees from the midlands brought a different link with the outside world, but this bit of North Devon seems to have remained rather isolated until after the war. As a result, I could hardly understand the dialect of these old boys, and they were very pleased to have a chance to pull the leg of "the young lady visitor".

"Avee ad a rabbut pay yer?" I was asked.

This being interpreted for me by my escort. I replied that no, I had not had a rabbit pie here. I caught a glimpse of twinkles exchanged between the four stalwarts who crammed the old settle. I was then solemnly assured that in order to make the pie, the rabbit must first be plucked.

"Plucked?" I queried, as was intended.

"Ar, plucked."

"What. Like a chicken?"

"Ar. Takes a long time. It do. Baint you nivver yerd of it, maid?"

"No, never," I said, and they all clicked their tongues and shook their heads sadly at the ignorance of town folk. I, too, exchanged a twinkle with my escort, and thereafter the evening proceeded with much good-natured banter. They put on their act of rustic simplicity. But they knew that I knew it. Never was there a truer saying – if you want to find a fool in the country, you'll have to take one with you.

I still remember that evening, when the dark old pub grew smokey and hot from the huge fireplace, before it was altered. The fire held half a tree trunk, and was backed up with peat cut from the moor. There was no fruit machine or billiards table then, just a dart board on the yellowed wall, and the shove ha'penny board.

When it was time to leave, we saw Fred Nash to his field gate. He was "nicely thank you" on a local brew which they wouldn't let me try, because it was too strong. (Shandy was considered more suitable for the young lady). Fred's legs were bowed to the shape of his horse and as he had impaired tear ducts in his eyes from a Great War injury, all his laughter was accompanied by tears. When well-oiled, he could imitate the cuckoo perfectly, and on that December night its summery cries floated back to us across the frosty fields.

Another "oldie" I remember is Donnie. He was here when I bought the cottage, and I am indebted to him for recommending Pentland Ivory as a good potato. He also pointed out a strange phenomenon in this village, which is that certain crops will romp away on one side of the river and fail miserably on the other. I proved this to be true with Home Guard potatoes. My crop was very meagre, but a neighbor who used a piece of ground not a hundred yards away, over the bridge, had bumper crops from this variety.

Donnie was small and slight, and always wore his cap. He lived in a caravan housed in a barn a couple of miles up the valley, and did odd-job gardening. He dearly loved his pints and when in funds, would arrive at opening time and stay in the pub to sleep it off on the settle till the evening session. As the night progressed Donnie would begin to sing his limited repertoire. Many surprised visitors have had Donnie's solemn face appear not a foot from their own, while he favored them with "push the damper in, pull the damper out, the smoke goes up the Chimney just the same."

Then his head would droop lower and lower over his glass and stay there until someone woke him with the welcome cry, "Drink up. Donnie!"

It was not unusual, I was told, for him to give up on his journey home in the summer and sleep the night away in the road-side hedge. When it got colder, someone would run him up the valley but I believe there were occasions when he wandered away from the pub on his own, and then a few of the men would take their torches and go in search of him. Always amiable never offensive. Donnie was missed in his corner when he died.

Times have changed here, as elsewhere and now one can no longer buy clotted cream at the farms, or freshly caught fish from local boats. Why the fishing should have died out I do not know, because we have to go twenty miles to a fresh fish shop, so I would have thought even a weekly catch would have paid off well.

The advent of the West Country holiday boom is partly responsible. Today's fishermen do better with boatloads of visitors taken for trips round the bay, while their wives do B and B. I was once invited to tea with an old fisherman and his wife, who lived near Shelley's cottage. (He lived in Lynmouth for a while). He summed up the local economy for me very neatly,

"Tis like this yer," he said. "When Visitors come in the spring until Easter, we go a bit easy-like. Then up to Whitsun, we puts it on a bit. And in the summer we robs 'em!"

Aunt May's is another face I miss. She lived in a cottage about five miles away, and before I bought mine I often used to come for a weekend and have B and B with her. She lived very simply and never went anywhere, but I always reckoned on catching up with all the local news when staying with her.

How is it done? I once had an old lady for a next-door neighbor and by means of leaning over the half-door in the front of her house, and accosting one and all, she became what my friends and I called "The Village Chronicle." When I arrived on a Friday she would wait to see me making the tour of my garden and then open her French doors.

"Good evening. Liz. Wayside Cottage is sold, and the birds have eaten all your raspberries."

To return to Aunt May; I treasure one of her pieces of news.

"'About the people staying in Farm Cottage. They've got a daughters Tis a, hair 'ostess".

When the evenings begin to draw in a little, I find myself using her words, "The nights are getting dimmy now".

Aunt May's brothers were all farmers, and one of them, retired and in his eighties, was staying with her when I went for B and B for a few days. Farmer Jack was still a fine upstanding man who was full of fun and liked to get about. After a couple of days he approached me with a proposition; if I would use my car to drive us both to the harbor starting-point, he would sport the fare for a steamer trip to Lundy Island.

This sounded like a good day out, and the next morning off we went. The sea was a bit rough and it was windy, but the trip along the coast showed me a different view of Exmoor. A surprising number of waterfalls cascaded down the cliffs and their great height could more truly be assessed from this angle. The Headland has a wide red gash on it noticeable for miles, and Farmer Jack told me that this was known as Great Red and he had climbed down it once to rescue a sheep.

We had been an hour late leaving the harbour and the tide was wrong for us to land on Lundv, so instead we cruised all round it. Lundv is home to all sorts of seabirds, including the puffin. and I was disappointed not to see a single one on its rocks. (I later learnt that they were all far out at sea in summer, returning to nest here in spring).

Farmer Jack and I tramped the deck, and ate sausage rolls, and drank the usual awful tea from the cafeteria, and thoroughly enjoyed ourselves. We had taken Tod coats with us and were glad of them. Once back on dry land we headed home, and at his request we stopped at a local hostelry to round off the day, and to buy a bottle of sherry for Aunt Mav.

It was dark when I parked the car in the shed for the night. It was a mini, and I went round to help Farmer Jack unfold his height and bulk from his seat. Grasping his stick he stretched upright dwarfing the mini and me.

"Well, I reckon that were a damn good day out," he said. grinning broadly "And I be going to kiss 'ee!"

And he did.

I later recounted this romantic interlude to a dear old friend mine. A maiden lady in her eighties. and expressed my surprise that a man of this age should still feel flirtatious.

"My dear," said Gertrude solemnly, "with men, no age is past it."

Have you ever had your coalman to lunch?

We specialise in nice coalmen here. There was Dicky, who used to lie down on the floor of the pub and beg someone to tell the rather slow barman that a customer had just died of thirst. Then there was Uncle, who brought his wife with him on his country rounds. And there was George who delivered one afternoon when I had made a curry for lunch.

“Yer, don’t that currv smell good, you," he exclaimed over the cup of tea he always had here. He confessed to a great fondness for it.

"Call in next week about one o'clock and you shall have one" I promised.

Sure enough, he did, and tucked into a steaming plateful, all the more welcome because the weather turned bitterly cold that day. I can't imagine doing this in a town, where you're lucky if you see the same delivery people twice. Here, everyone is a person, known by name, and that is how life should be.

Art groups and artists flourish in this locality, and I specially remember Elsie. She painted rather lurid landscapes of purple trees and orange clouds, but her portraits were first class. However, I really remember her for quite a different reason.

One Sunday, some neighbors invited her to accompany them to church. It was just after Christmas, so we were still singing carols. There were about ten of us in the congregation and we could give a good account of ourselves when it came to carols. But that day, as we began the chorus of "o come, all ye faithful", Elsie sang a descant.

It was a very high descant, and she sang it very loudly. She also sang it off-key, and wobbled on the top notes. We were all stunned – not least the couple who had brought her – but we struggled on, after being nearly silenced the first time it happened. When it came to the chorus a second time, we bowed our heads over our hymn books and dared not meet each other’s eyes. The third time, the lady organist played for all she was worth. Giving us fortissimo and double fortissimo to cover our shaking efforts, for we were all quaking with inner laughter and I know my face was scarlet with the effort of trying not to let it out.

I think there were four verses, and Elsie shrilled the descant to them all, after which the Rector (also suffering) promptly announced "Let us pray," and we all collapsed onto our knees and were able to cover our faces at last. That Sunday has become fixed in my mind as "The Day Elsie Sang."

You can't live in this village for long without encountering Tam. Maddening old man! His sheep stray everywhere. And he is not averse to opening a gate or lifting a piece of fence to let them in to a bit of grazing.

A few got into my vegetable patch one week and when Tam saw it on the Friday night it was scraped clean. Not unnaturally, I was very annoyed. All that work wasted, and all those goodies inside gorging sheep instead of appreciative me!

I went to see Tam and we exchanged a few irate remarks as he fell back on the old excuse of, "foreigners be always on about the sheep."

"Don't you call me a foreigner." I retorted. "I've known and loved these parts for thirty years and more."

I then went on to point out that some people would expect to be compensated, but that personally I would find a few logs a nice gesture.

"Logs?" said Tam. "You can't eat logs."

I never did get any, of course.

Not long afterwards he was sued by someone in the village and had to pay up, but his sheep still stray, and he gets away with it because you can't help liking him.

His clothes don't bear close scrutiny, and as they become ever more holey it is wise not to let one's gaze descend below his waist. He seldom shaves, and adopts from time to time strange head gear. Once he sported a bright orange knitted tea cosy for a hat. Last winter he had pink feathers from a feather duster stuck all round his hatband.

Two lady visitors will have cause to remember him. He backed his ramshackle car towards theirs and very slightly dented their bumper. Shambling round to look he told them, "Tidden nothun to worry about."

The ladies disagreed, and haughtily demanded his name.

"Aint got no name," Tam muttered.

"Well, you must live somewhere. What is your address?"

"No fixed abode," said Tam wickedly, and drove off – from right outside his own house.

He cheerfully admits that he didn't have much schooling, due to his frequent practice of sitting under a hedge all day instead of going into school, and returning home when the other children came out again. I'm not sure that he could even read or write properly, but Eva told me that he was very well-off.

Well, whether or not his sheep and his subsidies have made him rich, Tam is a sad old man now. His health is failing and he can no longer get about his fields. He sits in one room, by a Calor gas stove, with his faithful dog beside him, and not even a T.V. ("newfangled") for distraction.

The house on one side of me has had three different owners since I bought mine. At one time it belonged to a very pretentious couple who really were 'townies'. They dressed immaculately, she in the latest fashion, and he in mod styles which Tibs insisted on. Yes, I did say Tibs. I don't know what her proper name was. His was Nicholas, but – wait for it – she called him Kitkat! They were newly together, and they didn't stay long, but while here they afforded us much quiet amusement. They "dined" at night, when they came home from work with the curtains left wide open so that we might all see them seated at either end of a long table, with a candle in the middle.

They complained frequently... about smoke from my chimney, noise from the pub, horse droppings in the road, and insects in the shop. Tibs had a phobia about insects and hung yards and yards of net curtain over the French doors to keep them out. ("Oh, a bee, a bee!" She would cry), and one night I was entertained by a sight which I shall never forget.

It was one of those mild mid-winter nights when little moths are flying about, called, I think winter moths. They must have been attracted to the windows next door by the light inside the room. I was on my way up to bed, when a torch, flickering about in the dark, drew my attention to my landing window.

There in his garden was Nicholas, sent out in his pyjamas and dressing gown, running round on a moth-hunt, armed with the torch for spotting them, and a tennis racket with which to beat them down. I watched spellbound until I could no longer contain my mirth, and had to flee into my bedroom and collapse with shrieks of laughter muffled in my pillow.

Not many miles away, as the seagull flies, is a lonely beach, and here it was that I probably gave someone a good laugh.

You have to drive down a long farm track and leave your car at its end, from whence there is a long, long trail a-winding. The path skirts a field before entering the woods, and from then on it zig-zags through them, down the cliff face. You cross little springs and streams, and on a hot day the air is refreshingly cool, and scented with the ferns which grow thickly everywhere. As you drop lower and lower, the sound of the sea gets louder, and just as you think you will never get out of the trees and reach the shore, that is what you do. The woods stop dead, and you step out on to the pebbles. The waves are only a few feet in front of you.

Piles of lovely, bleached driftwood are strewn about, the pebbles are shaped like Easter eggs, of a pretty pinkish-grey colour, and there is no mess. What a delight in these days of pollution and litter habits! The small cove is protected by the curve of the wooded cliffs on either side, and you can't see a house anywhere. Only the wind and the waves and the occasional flock of seabirds disturb the solitude.

Here it was that I settled down for a picnic, one August Bank Holiday. The sky was Exmoor blue, the sun was hot, and the long walk had given me an appetite. But first – a dip in those lovely cool waves! No need to struggle beneath concealing towels to change into a swimsuit, because I was the only person for miles around. I wasn't sure of the currents, so I didn't go far out, but I splashed and wallowed happily.

Then I spread my towel on the pebbles got out my book, sighed with satisfaction, and enjoyed my picnic. What, I said to myself, giving the occasional glance at the sky and sparkling sea, could be better than this?

After lunch I had an idea. My swimsuit was taking its time to dry on me, and was beginning to feel a bit clammy...so I took it off. I abandoned myself to the sun and the warmth and gently, deliciously, fell asleep. Pink as a stranded mermaid I lay there deep in dreamless depths.

It was quite some time before the sound of the waves called me half back to consciousness, that, and a deep vibratory hum. The noise would grow louder and then fade again, as if some giant bumble bee were passing to and fro across the bay.

I shot back to life, looked up, and saw a helicopter hovering low overhead, the roar of its engine assaulting my now alert ears. Never was a towel more swiftly grabbed!

On a cold winter's day, I look back on my summer picnics, and on that particular one with a laugh. I'll bet someone else does, too!

Most country districts have their local "big house", and ours always puts me in mind of "Manderley" in Daphne Du Maurier's book "Rebecca". It is built on a plateau just above the sea, crowded by wood, and approached by a steep, winding drive three miles long, which is rough and difficult in winter. As you descend, the views are magnificent, with moors sweeping down to the trees, and the sea and wide skies ever-changing before and above you.

I was first taken there many years ago in late October. Having gazed in wonder at the exterior of the beautiful old house, bristling with curious tall chimneys, I almost gasped aloud at the inside. It was full of dark twists and turns, and stuffed with old treasures.

When we were shown into the library, the light bouncing in across the water, made a dazzling contrast. Books in their hundreds lined the walls, a huge fire crackled up the chimney, and tea was served in eggshell china. (By a uniformed maid, mark you. It was that long ago). My only recollection of the elderly lady who was fortunate enough to have inherited all this magnificence was that she wore bright green knitted stockings, and had the thinnest legs I have ever seen. They were like a sparrow's.

Fortunes change, and I assume that the cost of upkeep and repairs forced the present generation of the family to sell. We were all agog to know who would come forward with the necessary amount to buy the house. Rumors flew, but eventually it came into the hands of a multi-millionaire, who poured vast sums into its renovation.

He was self-made, and therefore all the antiques for which the house cried out had to be bought in. A local man was appointed agent, and sent out to auctions and dealers to gather pictures, furniture, silver, and curios by the ton. He was also told to go and buy a library, and the local joke was that he ordered the books by the yard. Any booklover will cringe at that. Books are for loving and collecting over a lifetime.

I was shown over the house by the housekeeper when it was finished, the new owner having flitted off to one of his four or five other places dotted about the world. It was different, but beautiful, and warm from new central heating. Large pots of orchids at £30 a pot, were scattered carelessly about; a baby grand, which no-one could play, had been installed; the yards of books were in situ, reflecting no particular interests or tastes, of courses; there were 'family' portraits of no one family all over the walls; there was a set of the most lewd and disgusting pictures hung in an out of the way corridor, for which purchase could only be (faintly) justified if they had been done by Hogarth. And there was, in one empty fireplace a pretty, dried flower arrangement in shades of white and pink.

"Guess how much that cost," said the housekeeper.

I peered more closely. Four of the ingredients grew in my own

garden. "About £10". I replied allowing for the florist's time and skill.

"Add another nought." she grinned. “And that doesn't include the pot."

I came away feeling rather sad. It seems all wrong that people can no longer afford to live where their roots go deep. "New" money has turned many a home into a showplace, saving the edifice, but changing the social pattern forever. This house isn't open to the Public, but how long will it be in today’s harsh economic climate before the funds dry up, the business empire tumbles, and the old place is up for sale again?

Its ghosts have already fled before the wind of change.

# Village shops

During my time at the cottage, the village shop has had five owners. Mary and Bert were the first I knew, and it was they who told me that the cottage was for sale, and put me in touch with Granny Kingsway, who owned it.

After them came Reg and Core. Reg had a crumbling spine, but his disability didn't dampen his sense of humor. We were always having digs at each other.

"Oh, just got up?" I would ask, when I went in at midday to buy something.

One afternoon he said that he would get David, his son to bring me a bag of coal across the road when they closed. I had been up my ladder clearing out the guttering, and, feeling rather grubby, I was in the bath when they opened the side gate.

"I'm in the bath," I yelled out.

"Where d'you want it put?" Reg called.

"Anywhere will do."

"Can't hear you! wait a minute-I'll come up the ladder."

Shrieks from me, and laughter below as he waggled the end of it by the window.

Then came a lively and mischievous young woman, who would appear behind the counter in mod clothes. When knickerbockers were all the rage, she wore them, and the local lads were reduced to dumbfounded goggling. I think there were a few flirtations, but she always made me laugh, and we used to go for long walks together. She was very kind to some of the older villagers, and patient with their fads.

Aunty Ida was one who somewhat tried this patience. In her eighties, she was so set in her ways that she always asked to have her potatoes "not more than three inches round, dear, please." And the tale of her trouble with the laundry still makes me laugh.

The shop was the agent for the local laundry, and we could drop our things in one week and collect them back the next. When the laundry changed hands, Aunty Ida was most upset to find that her sheets were now returned folded into a square, instead of the oblong she was used to.

"Would you ask the man not to do this, dear," she phoned. "I never have my sheets folded into squares. I don't like it at all. I have always had them the other way."

"Well, Aunty Ida, I think it would be much better if you spoke to the laundry yourself. Wait a minute, and I'll give you their number."

Half an hour later, Aunty Ida rang the shop again.

"I thought I'd tell you, dear. I rang the laundry as you suggested.

What a rude young man!"

The next owner of the shop was a man who came determined to alter the local tastes. Up on the shelves went all sorts of continental goodies, and the range of packet and frozen meals began to include pizzas, chow mien, lasagna, and the like. Up shot all the prices, too, but it was not entirely due to this that the "foreign stuff" was left on the shelves.

I could just imagine some of the older local farmers staring at their plates if their wives served up one of the new range of items.

"What's this, then? Damn me if it aint summat to make a pig sick, you"

After this we had a couple who proved to be the last of the line of our village shopkeepers. Generous to a fault, over-meticulous, often erratic in timekeeping, they never recaptured the trade lost by their predecessor. One winter the shop was closed, at only a week's notice, until Easter, and after that the offended locals turned their backs. A bad summer hit the tourist trade, at a time when the West Country was already struggling, and the deepening recession gave the coup de grace. Now we no longer have a village shop; it has joined the many other local businesses whose shutters have closed for the last time.

All the elderly ladies who haven't got a car now go to our nearest town on the weekly geriatric bus... and are pleasantly surprised at the supermarket prices.

# Happenings

So you think nothing ever happens in the country? Then how about these for headlines?

"Husband deserts wife and family for boyhood gay relationship".

"Wife gives job to woman who becomes husband's mistress."

"Father drops dead as bride leaves on honeymoon."

"Sheepshearer electrocuted."

"Villagers defy angry hunt and save stag on a roof."

Shame, treachery, tragedy, bravery... it is all here, as it is wherever people live together. We can never "get away from it all", because we take ourselves with us. But there are quieter headline on which I prefer to dwell.

"A feather falls." Straight from a circling buzzard overhead, it floated into my waiting hands. I have it still, brown and white, the shaft thick enough to make it into a quill pen, if I knew how, so it lives by an antique inkwell. Catching it gave me a strange feeling. There was the bird in the cold blue sky, and there was I, in the lonely combe, and the falling feather linked us for a moment in time.

"Monster seen on Exmoor." Yes, I really did think that I saw one, and my scalp prickled at the time.

I had gone for a long walk on the Chains, looking for Pinkery Pond. During the afternoon it grew overcast, and soon a wet, grey fog rolled in, obscuring the landscape. A farmer on horseback loomed out of it, and expressed concern.

"You'm going to get lost up yer maid" he said.

It was now beginning to rain, so I turned off down the rolling hillside, intending to make my way to the stream at the bottom, across it and up the other side to regain the moorland road eventually.

When I was halfway down the hill the grey mists lifted a bit, and I could look across to the opposite side of the valley. There, in the dim light of the late winter afternoon, I saw an enormous creature moving along. It was yellow, and I could make out numerous dark legs beneath it. It looked like a huge caterpillar, and I froze in my tracks.

Now, a caterpillar, however large, doesn't sound like something of which to be scared. But have you ever seen one all of twenty feet long? Up there, alone, with only the faint whistle of the wind and a curlew crying, and the light fading rapidly, I can tell you that it was a very eerie experience.

Suddenly a yellow piece of it detached itself and began moving rapidly down the slope, and headed in my direction. And I saw, thankfully, that it was human – a young lad with his yellow rain cape held over his head, and he came to check on their whereabouts. The other lads had all put their capes over their heads to keep off the rain as they followed a sheep track in a long crocodile.

I set their leader right, waved to the others, and made for the road home, and a strong cup of tea in the reassuring light of the lamps and the fireside.

There are rumours of a real live "Beast of Exmoor", but if there is any such creature -I don't want to know?!

"A calf is born". She was pacing a little patch of grass just over the hedge that borders the lane. Her great bulk seemed almost too heavy for her legs to support. As I paused, she lay down, and her sides heaved. In only moments, the birth being easy, I could see the calf's legs protruding from her rear, and then the bulk of its body and a small wet lolling head as it came free. The cow was on her feet almost immediately, licking the inert shape in the grass. I held my breath...it wasn't stillborn, was it? And then the little head lifted and wobbled for a moment.

That was in the morning. By evening, the baby was walking, his coat clean, dry, and fluffy. I had never seen anything born before.

It is pleasant, in the winter, to look back on such events. One sometimes sighs for the balmy days of summer, especially when it is your turn to do the church flowers and there is nothing in the garden. Or at least, nothing that one cares to pick, because "public" arrangements have always to be bold, and winter's flowers are mostly shy and small, though often sweetly-scented. One can get away with honesty and lichened branches and some sprays of brown oak leaves... perhaps a few still-clinging hips or haws to add colour. One can buy a few Chrysanthemums (cheating). Trails of ivy, polished with oil, make the most of a few precious snowdrops or polyanthus in a special corner. Bold branches of laurel contrast with sprays of spikey green broom, and show up well.

Christmas is easy, because then you can use berried holly and all kinds of evergreens, but "doing the flowers" in winter is challenging. The most memorable arrangement I have ever seen, beautiful in its simplicity, was just sprays of glossy un-berried holly mixed with pale yellow privet. I recommend this one to other "flower ladies" – I couldn't take my eyes off it.

I once found myself singing that I hadn't a big enough garden to make a special winter one. But then, when I looked around, I realised that I already had one! The arrival of each treasure's hour of glory is a great event in my winter calendar.

First, the pink viburnum Bodnantense covers itself with sweetly scented pink powder puffs. Then the Fairyland Tree sprinkles its branches with pink confetti. (This is properly called prunus subhirtella autumnalis roses, but my name is nicer, isn't it?) Next to it, a mahonia hangs its skeins of yellow flowers for weeks, from Christmas onwards, smelling strongly of lilies of the valley. A mild February day will find a daring bee visiting this bounty. In one corner, a laurustinus is flourishing most gratifyingly, grown from a cutting, and now generously covered in flowers which begin pink and age to white. Nothing daunts this brave shrub, which never looks pinched, however cold the weather.

Along the wall are dusky purple Lenten roses, helleborous atrorubens, and also some helleborous orientalis with greenish white flowers that are prettily freckled. These look like super Christmas roses, which won't grow for me – I've tried them three times. Another hellebore, lovely Corsicus, shows its apple green buds early, and I count them greedily every winter because I can never have enough of them. They glow, as if illuminated, against their dark and handsome leaves. These can get a bit brown and tatty-looking, here and there in winter, so I cut off the worst so as not to spoil the beauty of those pure clusters of saucer-shaped flowers.

The arbutus unedo will hang on to its strawberry-like fruits in a mild winter, but I am getting worried about its size. It is leaping up, and is clearly going to be a tree and not a shrub before very long, and then what is to be done? I prune judiciously, but I feel a contest of wills coming on.

Garrya eliptica is much more accommodating and is at last hanging out a respectable number of long green catkins, after years of struggling and moping. And overall, king of the winter garden, reign the Sunshine Bush, eleagnus pungens maculata. The colder it gets, the more he thrives and shines, and I look at him through a window framed in yellow jasmine and feel that lo, it is good.

However, like all gardeners, I get my troubles. My few winter heathers are a bit two-minded about staying, but sometimes one will put a spurt on. Springwood white does best for me. The mice eat the aconites and slugs nibble my iris unguicularis, and cyclamen coum will not stay and flower, though neapolitanum is happy here. But never mind, there are treasures in plenty in my winter garden, with more to come in snowdrop time – a sheet of honey-scented loveliness – and the arrival of each is a major event.

Some of the happenings in our village life shatter us with their sad suddenness. Who would have thought that Will, our semi-retired and ever busy clergyman, would die suddenly? But he did, and I miss him. He got my father's old clock going again for me, and whenever I wind it I think of his kindness.

And Eva...oh, how I miss her cheery smile and good common sense. Her house is still empty, and those blank windows give me a pang every time I pass. I know that I shall resent it when someone else comes to live there; it will seem all wrong. Meanwhile, the house-martins whose nests cluster thickly under the eaves have come and gone again, and she who loved wildlife is no longer with us to enjoy them.

Funerals are big events here, and the old custom is still kept of providing a tea afterwards. Nearly everybody goes, not out of morbid curiosity, but because this is a community, and we all know each other, if only by sight. The families of real locals don't hold with cremation. Jane, an elderly lady who has lived here for years, summed up the prevailing attitude when she said, "Cremation? There aint nothing in that-'tis 'alf way to 'ell on a conveyor belt to get burnt, and nothing left to show for it." So on these occasions one or other of the small local churches will be packed tight, and familiar faces look unusually stiff above collars and ties and dark clothes. The undertaker's men do their best, but they are not professionals, and sometimes there is a heart-stopping fumble.

Here I remember, with no disrespect, the funeral of Nolly-a dear, kind friend if ever there was one. He had a quick wit, and was never at a loss for the apt phrase. "I've just seen Rod coming home from the pub on automatic pilot," he once told me, and on another occasion, glancing up the road at a neighbor approaching on her old-fashioned bicycle, he smiled and said, "Ah, here comes Mrs. B. on her dromedary." So many attended the funeral of this well and widely liked man that there was barely room to manoeuvre his coffin at the end of the service. Even while I wept, I had to smile, because I could hear Nolly's voice saying, "Hello! I hope the buggers don't drop me!"

One snowy morning I decided to take the dog for a walk over the moors, so that I could enjoy them in their cold white majesty. There had been quite a fall, but now the skies were a clear pale blue and everything sparkled. The tiny stream at the side of the road was laced over with icicles and fantastic fronds of curling snow drifts.

I passed Abel on the way, his boots tied up as usual in plastic carrier bags to keep them dry.

"You'm off for a walk," he observed.

"Yes-going to get an appetite for dinner."

"Ar. Do 'ee like swedes, maid?"

"I certainly do," I replied. "I only wish I had space to grow a row. '"

"Never mind," he said mysteriously. "So do I, and there's more than one way to it." I puzzled over this cryptic remark for some time. Then I forgot it in the tingling pleasure of walking in the crisp air. It was glorious. All the hollows and bumps were smoothed out, and the snow crunched underfoot. There was a spring in one place which was buried in a long cavern of white, and when I bent to look, the icicles hung in crystal stalagtites, gleaming in the diffused light.

On the way back, I took a short cut. The usual track was buried deep under an untrodden glassy surface, where snow had melted and frozen again after days of bright sun and icy nights. The going was tricky, but I hate to retrace my steps, so I sat down and attempted to ease my way down the steep slope, using my heels as a brake. Too late I realised that it wouldn't work.

"Oh, I'm off!" I heard myself cry involuntarily, and down I flew, human toboggan careering straight to the stream at the bottom. Rick skittered after me, barking wildly, and together we arrived on the bank, where lumps of heather and whortleberry stopped us in the nick of time from an icy, watery drenching. This just goes to show that one should always treat Exmoor and its weather with great respect.

When I got home, there was a beautiful pile of earthy swedes on my doorstep. How good they tasted, freshly dug and cooked within the hour, and eaten with a winter-sharpened appetite!

*Liz frequently returned to this spot and recounted the story on this occasion she explained where one day her ashes were to be scattered'*

I bought Abel a drink when next I saw him in the pub, and thanks him profusely.

"Not a word," he muttered, digging me in the ribs and tapping the side of his nose. "Old Sturge ain going to miss 'em."

Old Sturge would not have been amused to know that Abel was not only raiding his fields, but giving away freebies as well.

Our scenery is so dramatic that it is often used as background to advertisements. Quite recently, while turning the pages of a glossy magazine, I found myself looking at a beautiful photograph of the village, taken from the top of the hill. There was the pub and the guest house, and there was my cottage. I could almost convince myself that a dark spot was myself in the garden, though I fear that it was only a drip from my coffee cup. The large red car, the raison d'etre for the advertisement was quite irrelevant.

It was rumoured that the owner of the field, seeing the activity when the photograph was being taken, hastened up and requested a fee...and got £50!

Much more exciting was the Gas Film.

Word went round that a T.V. crew was setting up all its paraphernalia a field above the village to make an advertising film, and we were all invited to take part as "extras". Up we all went on a very cold afternoon, and were quite piqued to see that hordes of "foreigners" had arrived from far away villages to take part as well. We cheered up when we were shunted into two groups and saw that most of these were in the half that had to go down to a cart track and walk along it in a long crocodile.(When the advert was shown on T.V- we were jubilant. "That lot" hardly appeared at all, and even then only at a distance!)

Our half was told to make a wide circle round an actor whose job it was to light the flame on a centre piece. As the flame swooshed up, we were all to step forward with excited expressions.

We practiced. We were all coming in too close. We practiced again. This time we were too fast. We did it again. We weren't looking excited enough. We did it yet again, and this time we got it right. Then the producer, or whatever he was, found that one of the spotlights hadn't worked, so we were told to sit down and wait while it was put right.

We waited for ages, and somebody's aunty was going blue with the cold, so I shot home and got her one of my coats. I arrived back just in time, as it was suddenly Action Stations, and Let's Go. One of the crew came round and for some reason measured a friend's ear, or at least, that was what he appeared to do. I put on a perfectly splendid, excited expression, the actor lit the flame, we all stepped forward, and that was that. We had "appeared" on television, and we were all paid £25 each for it.

We trooped homewards to thaw out, because it was now quite dark and we had been hanging about for hours. Whenever I see a scantily dressed cast in an outdoor advert on the box now, I pity them from the bottom of my heart and wonder if any of them subsequently died from pneumonia.

Three months later the film came up among all the other ads. In the intervals. It went so quickly that it took several showings before I could spot anyone I knew, let alone myself, apart from one close-up of Gwenny from the farm down the road. Then everyone started calling the friend whose ear had been measured "film star". We hadn't recognised him in the close-up, and even he scathingly remarked that "one of that other lot" must have shoved himself forward! My excited expression had gone unnoticed. Such is fame!

An annual event in our village life is The Sale. This used to be a pony sale, but I'm glad that it has become more of a general purpose one now. I hated to see terrified animals shoved about and shouted at, and I would never go near it. I'm glad that nowadays an RSPCA man attends, and the pony sale has dwindled considerably and is better conducted.

The rest of The Sale is a different matter. For days beforehand

the field steadily fills up with anything and everything; old cars, horse boxes, trailers, a pile of logs, rolls of old wire netting, buckets, kitchen units, washing machines, fridges...you name it, someone will put it in The Sale. The collection gets bigger and more varied every year, and some of it is junk. But it nearly all sells!

People wander round during the preceding days, just looking, and then on the day itself they appear from far and wide. There is an auctioneer to handle the proceedings and as he goes from item to item he is accompanied by a large crowd who greet all his sallies and asides with roars of laughter. There is a beer tent which is open all day, and that helps the conviviality along nicely. As darkness falls, sold items are driven away, and the singing from the tent gets louder. (And ruder, probably.)

I once put a chimney in The Sale.

During my struggles to achieve the best central heating for the cottage, of which more anon, I was advised to remove the old external brick Chimney. When it came down, I was also advised to put in its place a modern monstrosity. I did not know at the time that it would turn out to be this, which is one of the disadvantages of having work done when you are not resident in the property. Eventually, the monstrosity too was removed, and I put the hideous thing in The Sale, all twenty feet of its silvery ugliness.

I packed its separate, dismantled parts in a huge cardboard box, and a friend and I humped it by car into the field, where we left it with all the other items. I put a reserve price of £70 on it, and left it to its fate, as it began to pour with rain.

By the time the auctioneer had done his stuff, the box had disintegrated, and when all the sold items had been carted away, there my chimney sat in solitary state. Sadly, I collected it and brought it home, and stuck it back in the garden shed where it once again took up all the spare room.

I would love to have seen the buyer's face when he emerged from the beer tent at last, and found himself minus both his £70 and the chimney. Fortunately, someone had seen me take it away, and the next morning there was a very agitated chap at my door on the tick of nine o'clock.

He said he'd bought it, I said, "Thank goodness for that," and the matter was sorted out with laughter and handshakes. His relief was matched by mine as I saw him carry the thing up the garden and drive it away. After all, an enormous flue pipe is hardly the sort of thing you can give away as a Christmas present.

Quite a major happening stemmed from the day the loo got blocked up. Naturally, it happened on a Sunday when one can't get A Man to come and do something, and also I was still only here for weekends, so I had to leave it for a week. Hopes that it would magically right itself proved false, and I thought that the trouble was probably caused by the septic tank being overdue for emptying. I got out my deeds, but it was marked in two different places on separate maps.

I could roughly remember where Margie the previous neighbor, whose son fell in it had told me it was so I took my spade and began to dig. A day's work led to nothing, and I then went and asked various old established villagers if they knew where it was. No luck, and Henry confirmed my worst fears-that I would have to dig out the pipe all the way to the tank, starting at the down pipe on the cottage wall. This, with already blistered hands, I began to do. I left for my week's work with the garden beginning to resemble an opencast, coal mine.

During the week, a senior member of my profession commented on the state of my hands, so I told him what had happened.

"There's an easier way than that," he said. "You must try water divining. All you have to do is get a wire coat hanger, cut out the hook at the top, and cut through the bottom bit. That will give you two L-shaped pieces. Put a plastic penholder on each short bit to make handles, and walk about with one in each hand. When you stand over the pipe, the long ends will swing towards each other and cross. So you just walk the line and keep them like that. They won't move until you've passed the septic tank, so you'll be able to fix its position. Easy!"

I looked at him very doubtfully indeed.

"Try it," he urged. "I shall come back next week to hear how you got on."

I wasted a whole Saturday on "water-divining". True, the long arms of the cut coat hangers wiggled about, and I don't think it was the wind. But sometimes they would wiggle in one spot, and then not wiggle in the same one. I approached the area from different angles. I took my wellies off, in case they were interfering, as I once read that a water-diviner is stymied if you stand him on a rubber bathmat. Then I glanced up and saw a curtain twitching madly in a nearby house, so I gave up, went in, and had a whisky. Word would no doubt go round the village that I had gone mad.

To this day, I don't know if I was the victim of leg-pulling, especially as my colleague never came back to enquire.

In the end, my digging led me to the tank, much deeper than I had anticipated. I had been encouraged to carry on when I went to see old Mr. Stockom Someone told me that they had remembered it was he who built it, years ago.

"Er's deep," he said reflectively. "Let me see now-'tis a while ago, mind. But the pipe...ah, that's it, 'er do goo a bit to the left first of all, then 'er do goo stret on to the tank, and tis rit be the 'edge."

Sure enough it was right by the hawthorn hedge. I had it emptied filled in the excavations, and after four weekends without one, was at last able to use my loo again. A trowel up on the moor on a freezing January morning, surrounded by curious sheep, is no substitute.

Jumble sales and car boot sales make a constant round of local happenings. I have never known another place in which there are so many. Where does all the stuff come from? There must be a vast pool of junk which circulates in ever widening circles, as it is bought, taken home, and given away again. I have a feeling that if one waits long enough, that ugly old glass sugar bowl which one thankfully donated, will reappear some day and stare one in the face accusingly from a local stall.

I only help at one jumble sale, as I was put off forever at my very first attempt. They gave me the white elephant stall, and I tried to tidy it up a bit. There was a great pile of something which looked like an endless bandage, so I started to roll it up neatly.

A toothless old crone appeared and stood there watching me.

"I can't imagine what this is," I said chattily, busy rolling.

The gums widened into a hideous grin. "It's a flannel binder, dear," she cackled.

Yuk!

The stall on which I now help once a year is good fun. A whole street is closed to traffic in a local town, and every charity and good cause you can think of has a pitch there. Our stall belongs to a society which works to abolish deer hunting, and we get crowds of people eager to buy and support this aim. We sell a wide range of items, including plants and home-made cakes, and when the day is fine and the hurdy-gurdy is playing, the atmosphere is quite festive.

Usually we get a fine day, but one year it poured all the time and we all got soaked. To make matters worse, I inadvertently parked the wrong side of a beastly little red cone, and when I squelched back to the car I found a soggy note tucked on the windscreen, demanding a fine of £15.

Last year, I made a batch of gingerbread cakes for the stall, and packed them up, prettily labelled, in white doilies and cellophane. My first customer was a pleasant lady who said, as she handed me I her 40p., "I'm sure I shall enjoy that."

"I'm sure you will," I agreed "I made them myself from a very old recipe."

Fifteen minutes later, I let out a shriek which startled all my fellow jumble-sellers.

"My cakes!" I cried. "I've just realised-I forgot to put the ginger in!"

I shot round the stall, to gales of laughter, and changed all the labels to "Treacle Cake". I still feel guilty when I think of that nice customer. I wonder what she feels when she thinks of me and my very old recipe.

Occasionally, "the pictures" come to the town hall not far away. This is an amusing event, especially if the film to be shown is more traditional and not one of today's wierdies.

The show will usually be billed to start at 7.30p.m. By 8.0 o'clock the whistles, stamps, and vocal comments have reached a crescendo. Then a harassed official comes in and tells us that the van, which had broken down on the way, has now arrived, and the projectionist is nearly ready. (Loud cheers.) The lights go out, and then come on again. Somebody calls out, "Programmes, chocolates, cigarettes."

(Laughter and slow handclaps.) The lights go out again, and the screen begins to show a series of flickering lights and numbers, and the claps turn to a genuine round of applause.

When the title comes up, it is not infrequently the wrong one. More delays, and a surge of restiveness like a giant wave sweeps through the hall. The official reappears, and asks if we would like a cartoon while the projectionist gets the right film out of his van? We certainly would, and to yells of approval, Donald Duck swaggers across the screen. He is followed, after thunderous applause and shouts of "MORE: " by Mickey Mouse.

After that, we usually set the film we have come to see. The local wits pepper it with their comments, and love scenes are apt to cause either ribald remarks or outbursts of theatrical weeping, but it is all good fun and an event not to be missed in the calendar of our winter days.

One winter we had an unusual number of gales, and one of them had a whirlwind effect in the valley and did a lot of damage. Half a wood disappeared on a hillside where the winds hit the coast, and trees were splintered like matchwood. As the storm raged up the valley, one tree after another was wrenched down, and the scared occupants of one house lost count of the crashes in the wood just above them. When morning came, the scars were pitiful to see. Fortunately no-one was hurt, but few sights are sadder than a noble old fellow laid low, his roots exposed and his branches smashed, no longer home to squirrels, birds, and countless insects.

A newcomer to the valley has been named Slasher, because he is never happier than when wielding a chain saw. People should have to get a permit – and then only with difficulty – before they can cut down a tree. Who are we to cut down what has usually taken more than our lifetime to grow?

High tragedy has stuck the steep North Devon coast more than once. Everyone knows about the terrible storm which, in 1952, devastated the pretty little village Lynmouth. Not quite so many know about the ferocious. January gale in 1899 which prevented the launching of the local lifeboat, when a ship was in distress out in the bay. A plaque on the wall of the building, which now stands on the site of the old lifeboat station, pays tribute to what happened, and beneath an old barometer is written;

"This barometer, provided by the Royal National Lifeboat Institution, is placed here to record the epic launching of the Lynmouth lifeboat from Porlock on the 12th January 1899, to the

"Forrest Hall" of Liverpool, and in memory of 2nd Coxswain W.H. Richards, youngest and last surviving member of the crew, also harbour master of Lynmouth for many years."

No event since that one has been writ larger in the pages of our local history. An account appeared in the RNLI's house magazine, The Lifeboat, in November of that year, of which a copy is appended.

The surnames of some of the crew are still to be found locally;

J.Crowcombe (Coxswain)

G.S.Richards (Second Coxswain)

R.Ridler (Bowman )

R.Burgess

G.Rawle

J.Ward

W.Jarvis

C.Crick

B; Pennicot

D.Crowcombe

T.Pugsley

W.Richards

**<u>1st NOVEMBER, 1899.THE LIFE BOAT,</u>**

*Lynmouth, North Devon. -Telegrams were received at about 7 Pm. on' the 12th January asking for assistance to a vessel showing signals of distress of' Gore Point. Almost immediately after the messages had been received the wires were blown down and it was impossible to obtain any further information. A whole gale was blowing from W.N.W., the weather was thick and the sea so heavy as to render it impossible to launch the Life-boat Louisa, at Lynmouth. It was therefore decided to take the boat on her carriage 'by road to Porlock.*

*Those who are unacquainted with the nature of the road between Lynmouth and Porlock can form but little idea of the immense difficulty of the undertaking.*

*The course taken was over two of the steepest hills in England, the road rising 1500 feet in two miles; in parts of the route the Life-boat had to be taken on skids, the carriage being taken through fields, gates and posts having to be pulled down, the road ,being too narrow for the wheels to pass, and the men were obliged sometimes to hold , and at other times to hold the boat back, so that their strength was greatly taxed. The undertaking even in daylight would be beset with danger to life or limb, but on a dark and stormy night, when it was difficult for a man even to stand in exposed places, it was only just possible to accomplish the work. However, in the uncertainty as to the danger to the vessel and in the absence of any other means of getting to her, it was decided to make the attempt. Horses were procured and the crew with twenty-eight helpers started with the Life-boat. The journey, which occupied ten and a half hours, ended without casualty, and at six o'clock 'on the following morning the Life-boat was launched at Porlock and proceeded to the vessel, which proved to be the full- rigged ship Forrest Hall, of and for Liverpool, from Bristol in ballast, 1900 tons register, with a crew of fifteen men; she was lying at anchor disabled. It appeared that she had been in tow of a steam-tug, and when westward of Ilfra combe the hawser parted and the tug collided with her and disabled the steering gear. Shortly after the arrival of the Life-boat two steam-tugs came up and took the ship in tow, the Life-boat men assisting to get the anchors up, and the Life-boat remaining by her, as she was in an unmanageable state owing to the loss of her steering gear, besides which the weather had become very had. She was ultimately towed to a safe anchorage outside Barry, and the Life-boat crew, who had been without food for twenty- four hours, landed at Barry Dock to obtain refreshment. On the following day they returned to their station, a steamer kindly giving them a tow part of the way, arriving there at 11.30 am.*

*The carriage was brought back by road, having covered a distance of twenty—eight, miles.*

# Power Cut

Today, after a gale in the night, we awoke to find that a tall alder tree had crashed across the river, bringing some cables down with it. Some of us still had our electricity, but it had to go off for most of the day as the gang of men toiled to put things right.

Out came all my first line of defence works.

I keep a candle and matches in every room as a matter of course, but I also have two Tilley lamps, a Calor gas lamp, a gas camping stove for cooking (one saucepan at a time), various torches, and that great ally – a good fire.

One learns to keep all these items at the ready in winter, together with extra candles, plenty of matches, spare mantles for the lamps, a bottle of methylated spirits (also for the lamps, not for sinister drinking), firelighters, canisters of gas, and the coal scuttle always well-filled. The lamps have to be tried out early on in the winter to make sure that all is in working order.

I have only recently discovered just how good an ally the fire is. It was on one of those occasions when the power had to be off for routine maintenance work on the line. It was due back on at four o'clock, so lunch was easy – a sandwich – but I craved my coffee. It seemed such a fag to get the little stove out of its box and set it up to boil a drop of water. I looked at the fire, glowing redly, and suddenly remembered the war years.

Many were the kettles and saucepans of soup and stew which our undaunted mothers simmered on the sitting room fires in those grim days of bomb-damaged power supplies. In no time at all, my smallest saucepan was nestled onto the red coals, and it boiled unbelievably quickly. So, today, I squeezed two into the grate, and cooked my lunch there on. I shall be searching the hardware stores and ironmongers for a good old-fashioned trivet to facilitate matters in future.

Making toast, you would think, presents no problem, but not so. First of all, if you are out of home-made bread, shop bread is wobbly. It has no guts. You prod it on to the toasting fork at a slight angle and start it off over the fire, but take your attention away for a second and a hole will appear and you are left with the slice dangling perilously. Or you forget how intense the heat is, and just as you smell scorching, it goes up in flames or Patch decides that this is the moment to show canine affection, and shoves her nose in your face, and in fending her off, you drop the lot into the fire. And then there is Sam. He will spy the butter dish warming in the grate, and like most cats he is partial to butter...

I usually do without toast.

The river has been well over its banks all day, flying and roaring along, and the rain has been coming in heavy storms. At three o'clock, Ben's mane was soaked so I decided to get him in early. I rattled his bucket and he arrived at the field gate. Then he took one look at the gang of men milling about round their generator and lorries and shot off up the field.

An hour later, I tried again. The other Exmoor pony, with whom he is at present sharing the fields, has been in all day, awaiting the blacksmith, and Ben does not like solo treatment. Inch by inch, I lured him on with pieces of carrot. Then the man working up the nearby pole, in a sort of yellow bucket on a crane, started to be lowered to the ground. Ben skidded to a halt and snorted. After a few gyrations he ended up sideways-on. I shoved the bucket of goodies over his nose, and greed, thank goodness, took precedence and he scuttled round to his stable. Getting Ben in on his own can be quite nerve-racking.

Fortunately the day hasn't been cold so the men haven't had too bad a time of it. In bitter weather of snow and ice, when the lines are down and the yellow helicopter zooms up and down looking for breaks, they are heroes, everyone.

More defence works come out in very severe weather, when one cannot use the central heating because the power is off. I have three Calor gas room heaters and three paraffin oil heaters, so supplies for these must also be got in before the winter begins.

Life in the country – real, isolated country – is quite different from city life. In times of crisis it is harder, less convenient, but – curiously – more satisfying.

Keeping oneself and one's house warm, and all comers substantially fed, whether they come on two legs, four legs, or wings, is a daily challenge, but one has laid in plenty of extra food stuffs for all.

My only lack is the means to have a deep, hot bath at the end of each freezing day, but a big maslin pan of water, made really hot on the fire, together with kettles singing on all stoves, provide enough for a shallow quick bath. What I should really like is an old-fashioned galvanised one to use by the fire. Remember those? I haven't seen one for years. I can dimly recall being bathed in one as a child when we had very cold weather, with the cosy warmth of the fire on one side, and the clothes horse draped with warming towels on the other to keep off the draughts. I felt like a pampered princess, and I should dearly love an old "tin bath" again, for emergencies.

When in the midst of a power cut, we glean bits of news and pass them on to each other.

"Ron says nobody's got power this side of the moor."

"About thirty-six hours for us... Nigel got a Land rover up to where they're working, and that's what they told him."

"That's if we don't get another blizzard," says the Village pessimist.

We battle on.

Well, today's was only a minor crisis and there have been no ominous flickers since the power was restored. The wind dropped, so I don't think I shall have to camp by the fire tonight, minus an electric blanket. Soft and romantic as candlelight is, there is a sense of relief when the bright light floods out again at the flick of a switch.

After a major crisis, I feel like cheering when everything works again. It is as if the village, like Mafeking, has been relieved.

# Saga

This is not the Saga of the Age, which would sound more poetic. This is an account of my trials and tribulations with Rayburns, upon which I can now look back and laugh.

When I bought the cottage there was, in the kitchen, a big old-fashioned one, creamy beige in colour with a rusty black back and a shelf above it for holding plates and saucepans. The smoke went up a length of black flu pipe, and through a hole in the wall into the old exterior brick chimney. Someone in the village said that she believed it still worked and would give hot water, and she would ask her husband to call in and look at it.

Her husband came. We lit a fire in it. No hot water arrived after the appropriate time, and David said that he thought there was an airlock and he would be back "dreckly" and sort it out.

Now, as I think I have said before, when the locals promise to come directly you are usually lucky if you see them again inside a fortnight. David was the exception and arrived with a hose pipe the next morning.

As time went by I got quite used to having a flood in my kitchen, but this was my first. Under David's administrations, water shot everywhere, and the more he wrestled with his hose pipe the more the water flew about. Once one was thoroughly wet it became interesting to see what that hose pipe would do next. At last he yelled to me to “turn the bugger off", meaning the stop-tap, so I did, and he went home to his dinner and I mopped up, and forgot to have mine.

In the afternoon he came back again. Clearly he was made of sterner stuff than would allow a simple piece of rubber pipe to get the better of him. We were now going to turn on all the taps which, should be hot taps and drain the system. It took a long time, but we sat and drank tea and gossiped agreeably until there were only drips left. Then he took that hose pipe and rammed it brutally on to the cold tap in the kitchen sink. Had it been a serpent he would have wrung its head off. The other end went somewhere into the bowels of the hot water storage tank.

The cold-water end only slipped off once, and the fountain of spray which errupted when he jammed it back on again was nothing compared with the morning's cascades. All sorts of gurgling noises went on in the tank, and at last David expressed satisfaction and gave it as his opinion that 'Er might now do. (Why are recalcitrant pieces of equipment always either 'er or she?)

The hose was removed and dropped on the floor, where it emptied itself from both ends in a steady trickle to form a nice little puddle. David went up in the loft and said that the tank was filling up nicely and we would now light a fire in the Rayburn. Twenty minutes later he tried the hot tap and said triumphantly, "'Er's tepid." We later celebrated with a whisky or two in the pub.

That was my first skirmish with the Rayburn. Thereafter it gave plentiful hot water and warmed the kitchen beautifully, but cleaning out its ashes made an awful lot of dust, and there were times when the direction of the wind caused it to send out billows of smoke. I was forever cleaning the shelves and window sill, and I resolved that one day, when I lived here permanently, I would have a new and modern version, and hopefully no more smoke and dust.

There was one weekend when the water increasingly turned a funny colour and had a nasty smell. I went up in the loft with a torch and looked into the tank, and found a dead bird decomposing in it. I fished it out sadly, found a piece of hardboard to make a cover, and ran the bath water until it once again came out clean and fresh.

There was also a mystery...an occasional strange booming noise, just like a sonic boom. It would rattle the windows, and it wasn't until years later, when I had a new tank in the loft to replace the ancient galvanised one, that the plumber came up with a possible explanation. He said he thought that, when I ran a bath, the sides of the old tank sometimes buckled, and then the in rush of cold water forced them out again, and caused the booming noise. I was lucky, he added, that gallons of water hadn't descended through the ceiling, because the tank was so old that 'er could have burst. ('Er again.)

I remember, too, the night when the water got to boiling point in all the pipes. I awoke in the small hours to frightening rumbles and bumps, as I imagine an earthquake must sound, and what prompted me to turn on the hot tap in the bedroom washbasin I don't know. My Guardian Angel, possibly, who must have been flapping his wings like mad to cool down in the kitchen.

At first, only steam came out, hissing fiercely, and I expected the cottage to blow up at any moment. I went down and shovelled out some of the Rayburn's red coals, and put them, also hissing, in the garden, but beyond that I couldn't think what to do, except to turn on every hot tap in the house.

Presently the steam turned into drips and then a trickle, and then boiling water gushed out, and I let it run away until it was only hand-hot, and breathed a sigh of relief. A crisis had been averted. I made a cup of tea and went back to bed for the rest of the night. I expect my G.A. winged his way wearily back on the long flight to wherever good angels go, shaking his head over the follies of humankind.

These incidents apart, Old Faithful served me well, if dustily, for a number of years.

Then I heard of a second-hand Rayburn which was being removed from a local cottage, on offer for a fiver. It, too, was one of the old cream-colored models, but it was newer than mine and in much better condition. I was pleased to get it, and a young man delivered it, removed the old one, and installed its successor.

Mike was immensely strong. He needed very little help to manoeuvre the heavy things, and the job was done in a day. Who would have thought that this fresh-faced, cheery young country lad would, before many years, waste away and die of cancer? I feel sad when I think about it.

Rayburn number two caused much less dust and smoke, and its innards were all in working order, so I could use the oven. Local women assured me that food always tasted better from this kind of cooking, so I experimented. I mixed up a rice pudding and left the dish in while I went out for the day. I dearly love rice pudding, especially the crisp brown baked bits on the top.

Crisp brown baked bits was all that was left of my pudding when I came home. The rest of it had cooked away, as the oven was too hot. So I tried putting a vegetable casserole in it overnight, as – mindful of over-heating – I was now always careful not to make the fire up too much at bedtime. It was very nice indeed. The only trouble was that it was ready at breakfast-time, and though I can eat a wide assortment of things at this meal, vegetable casserole is not one of them.

Shortly after this Rayburn arrived, so did my second flood in we kitchen. It is not nice to come down in your night attire on a cold dark winter's morning and step straight into an inch of cold water. Such things are apt to make one address the world in hard, bitter and highly-colored words.

It took me three quarters of an hour to mop it all up. (Later on, experience enabled me to it down to half an hour.) Then I tried to find out what had happened. The Rayburn was dry as a bone, all the tanks were all right, and so were all the pipes. There were no wet patches on the ceilings, so I drew a blank. For the next few nights I slept uneasily, and got up to look at the kitchen, but all was well, so gradually I pushed it to the back of my mind.

Flood number three happened almost exactly a year later. In those days I hadn't carpeted the sitting room, but had hair cord on the floor, and it only took two days to dry out, where the water had seeped through from the kitchen. But, clearly, I must solve this soggy mystery. I adopted a process of elimination I ran each sink and washbasin tap in the house for five minutes, and stood waiting

in the kitchen to see if anything untoward happened. Nothing, dry as dusts. Then I ran some bathwater, pulled out the plug, and hastened downstairs.

Soon the culprit was flowing in under the back door, and I flew outside with mop, bucket and broom and found the cause. Bath-water from the downpipe ran straight into a small drain, and the previous evening's gale had blown a pile of dead leaves into it. The rush of bathwater had flattened them into a waterproof lid, so it all overflowed, first into the porch, and then under the door and over the step into the kitchen Thereafter, I always checked that it was clear last thing at night, and I put a piece of slate over it as well to keep the leaves out.

Two things happened before the fourth flood. I got Will, the builder whose red tulips still come up and flower every spring, to replace all the old lead pipes in the house with copper ones, and I also asked him if the Rayburn could be made to run a radiator on the upstairs landing.

Will said it could, and he fixed me one. This was very cosy, and I looked forward to the time when I could afford full central heating in preparation for my retirement and permanent living at the cottage.

The second event was a new carpet for the sitting room, wall to wall, of a rich golden colour, subtly mottled with green and dark amber, so that one could not see a pattern but was aware of the shading. It was called "Shadows", and I was lucky in that having looked at it one day and left it until the next before deciding to buy it, the shop started a sale and I got it for £70 less.

We all love a bargain. Unfortunately, I wiped mine out the same week by scrunching the wing of the car against a pillar in a car park.

However, the carpet looked lovely when it was down. Three weeks later, it was draped inside a neighbor's shed, dripping steadily.

Flood had struck again, and this time the wet ceiling and damp floorboards gave the culprit away immediately. The landing radiator was leaking. Will was a builder rather than a plumber-and-heating expert, and he had put in the radiator to oblige me. It was the man in the builders' merchant store who explained matters.

"I can sell you another radiator," he said, "but in a year's time the same thing will probably happen again, and then you'll be after my blood. You need a separate tank in the roof, and an indirect system for central heating."

This was not fair. It was hitting below the belt. I had come to grips with septic tanks, stop cocks, bunged-up loos, and thwarted bath water. Now here was this man talking glibly about indirect systems.

I once saw a T.V. play about a woman who felt that she had become a non-entity in her middle years. Her children had grown up. Her husband had his work and his golf. What had she got? Only the W.I. and jam-making, so she hired herself to a local builder who had advertised for an odd-job person. After a struggle and a brush with the Equal Opportunities people, he had to give her the job. She got all the rotten tasks, but her doggedness and willingness to learn earned his grudging respect in the end. Then she dumbfounded her family by announcing that she was going to put in their central heating herself.

There were rows. There was ridicule. There was unexpected backing from the builder, who told her what to buy. And she did it. The long, slow smile of satisfaction on her face as the radiators warmed and the water ran hot was a brilliant portrayal of what I know I would feel myself if I had been clever enough to achieve the same thing.

I, however, came home from that discussion at the builders' merchants (What a nice, helpful man, I thought. Then.), and gave matters serious attention.

There were five years to go before I retired to live permanently at the cottage. I intended to have a new Rayburn and full central heating when that time came. Why not have it now? I missed that cosy warmth from the upstairs radiator, and I felt that the novelty had worn off floods in the kitchen, after the fourth one.

I got the plumber to give me an estimate, looked at my bank balance, and decided to go ahead. And if you think that I'd had my troubles, you aint heard nothing' yet.

I went to the same builders' merchant, sought out the same man, and said that I had decided to go the whole hog now instead of in five years' time. Please would he show me some new Rayburns?

We descended into the bowels of the earth to look at them. There was a sparkling white one in a corner, with smart chrome trim. It had a dial on the front which gave the temperature, and other refinements, and although I looked at others, and other colors in the catalogue, this was the one I chose. I half-expected to buy it and have it delivered the next day, but it had to be ordered. I was promised prompt delivery, and left it to the man to let the plumber know when it would arrive at the cottage.

In preparation, a young builder dismantled the old brick chimney. It was beginning to pull away from the wall, and could become unsafe. In its place I was advised to have "the finest chimney money can buy," so it was ordered. My neighbor, Den, had all the old bricks and rubble as hardcore for the garage he was building.

I arrived one Friday to find the new chimney in place, and I hated it on sight. This was the enormous silvery flu pipe which eventually went in The Sale. It was totally out of keeping with my dear little cottage, and I immediately began to think how I could case it in and hide it. Then I went indoors, and there was my new white Rayburn snugly in its place.

There was also, on the top of it, a large notice in capital letters, saying "DO NOT USE."

I assumed that the plumber hadn't quite finished connecting it up, but the next morning the young builder, who was liaising with him, called in.

"Why can't I use it?" I asked.

"Well," said Denis.

"Well what?"

He lifted the hot plate off and showed me a crusting of white inside. Running a finger along, he licked it, and said "It's salt. They had a flood in the basement and this has been under tidal water."

I was dumb founded. Closer inspection revealed pockmarks all over the inside of the oven door, the temperature guage had obviously come loose and been put back crooked, and the innards of the thing were still damp. I thanked the young many and said that I would Deal with It.

And deal with it I did. Sizzling with rage, I was on the doorstep of that builders' merchant by half-past eight on the Monday morning. I demanded to see the Managing Director, or whoever was top man, at once. The receptionist, after one startled look, whisked me up to his office. He looked like Mr. Pickwick, and I looked like what I was – one very angry woman. How dared they try and pull a fast one on me?

Mr. Pickwick sent for That Man, and said that he had given instructions that nothing was to be sold which had been in the flooded basement. I said that the wet Rayburn had to be out of my cottage that same day. He said he couldn't promise. I said it would be put out in the road if they didn't. He agreed. I said I would reluctantly order another one. That Man said they had now gone up. I said I would only have it at the old price, (Mr. Pickwick looked daggers at him), and also that they would have to pay the plumber for the extra work incurred. Mr. Pickwick agreed.

Round one to me.

Eventually, another white one was delivered and installed, and I felt that at last my troubles were over. It had cost nearly £1000, but it certainly did look smart. I lit the fire in it, and in no time at all I had hot water and lovely warm radiators all over the house. I decided to use the hot plate to heat some milk for a cup of coffee, and I stood there watching it and warming myself happily.

Suddenly there was a sharp crack. I looked everywhere for the cause, and it was not until I passed a damp cloth over the top, to remove some dust, that I found it. A tiny hairline of little bubbles appeared in one place, marking the spot where the top had cracked.

Distraught, I rang up the plumber.

"Oh, that'll be where they've screwed the top on too tight at the works," he said. "don't worry. They'll send another top."

At the company's expense, they did, and paid for it to be fixed.

About a month afterwards, I wiped it with a cloth and took a handful of the black enamel away with it. Could one believe one's eyes?

Alas, one had to. Correspondence with the company was exchanged, and I was advised that the manufacturer's engineer would come and inspect it. He came, and could find no fault, either with the appliance or with the chimney, which also was scrutinised. Another new top would be sent.

It came. Before long, the same thing happened again. (You can hardly believe all this, can you? Neither could I.) Back came the engineer, and this time diagnosed the cause of the trouble. When the Rayburn went out each week, condensation formed in the chimney and seeped down, and its acid nature ate into the enamel and caused it to flake off. How ironic that this had never happened with the good old-fashioned brick one! So much for "the finest chimney money could buy?"

"These things are meant for continuous burning," said the engineer. Scenting trouble, I told him that the suppliers knew that I was not yet living permanently at the cottage, and if this was the case they shouldn't have sold it to me.

I went to see them, and Mr. Pickwick said that as long as anything went wrong, it would be out right, so I said that I would have a complete new model, and they agreed.

Well, that, too, came and was put in, and very gingerly. I lit Its fire, and thought that surely nothing else could go wrong? Cautiously I opened the fire door to check that the sticks and coal were burning up nicely. I didn't trust it, you see.

And then...then...THEN, in a tiny twinkle of brightness alighting on the floor by my feet, there lay a piece of white enamel, off the door.

That was it. I had had enough of Rayburns going in and out of my cottage like peas from a pod. A long battle ensued, involving the trading standards officer and a visit to my solicitor, but in the

end I won. They came and took it away, and I got my money back.

Before I pass on to happier things, I will utter a word of advice, Always put everything in writing, and always keep a copy. I had several wakeful nights when I realised that I might not be able to prove, if necessary, that the suppliers knew I wasn't permanently in residence. It had all been verbal. So write and confirm things, keep your copy and don't lose your evidence!

I was now left with a gaping hole in the kitchen wall, an empty space, and a chilly house. To make matters worse, when I started to ask around the village as to what kind of heating other people used they all seemed to have Rayburns which never gave any trouble and which they said they wouldn't be without, so where did I go from here?

I began to delve. The more I delved – into magazines, brochures, heating advisory centres and the like – the more bewildered I got. Indirect systems were as nothing compared with BTU'S, and all the other technical jargon with which I struggled. There were back-burners, self-feeding hoppers, wood-burning stoves, coal-burning stoves, and multi-fuel stoves. There was coke, house-coal, anthracite, smokeless fuel, brickettes and nuts.

"Oh, nuts to you," I said, chucking the last brochure on to the floor. "Why can't coal be just coal? Why can't I live in a tent down the garden and cook in a pot hanging over a fire?"

"Because they would come and take you away to your padded cell if you did," said the friend to whom I was moaning.

I thought that the wood and solid fuel stoves were worth considering, so I sent for more brochures and was called on by an assortment of reps. How charming and persuasive they were! Some of them were quite pretty (the stoves, not the reps), and so were the prices. They all said how nice their own particular company's model would look in a cottage kitchen.

Only my long-suffering Guardian Angel could have directed me towards a local firm, who sold various company's stoves, but also made one themselves.

The boss-man came to see me at the cottage on a Saturday morning, took one look at the kitchen, and said, "You'll roast! You'll have to have a grating cut in the ceiling to let some of the heat escape upstairs. I can't sell you one."

Oh blessings on him! "If a virtuous woman has a price beyond rubies, so has an honest man. I wrote him a heartfelt letter of gratitude after his visit, because although I was nearer to a solution of my problem, he had saved me from a another very costly mistake.

But help was at hand. Wafted in, surely, by the energetically waving wines of my G.A., the young builder, Denis, called again.

"Why don't you have Calor gas central heating?" he asked casually. "All you'll see is a little box on the wall, and four red gas bottles in the garden."

My jaw dropped. I stared at him. Wasn't he shining with some strange, unearthly glow?

"You won't even need a chimney," he added. "You'll just have a small vent in the outside wall."

Yes-definitely. He was gleaming with a heavenly radiance. He was positively illuminated.

"You mean that horrible thing can be taken down?"

He nodded. "A pal of mine installs Calor heating. I'll ring him up and ask him to call."

I am almost ready to write "happy ever after."

Some workmen nipped in and took down the chimney at short notice for Denis' pal to come and do the job. They left the bottom bit that went through the wall, and I hacked this out myself. It expurgated my hatred of the thing to bash and gouge with hammer and chisel. When the neat little box was fixed up on the kitchen wall, it left me with a useful corner for two wide shelves and storage space below. I tiled the wall, and couldn't believe that so happy a solution had so suddenly fallen into place.

There was no more smoke and dust. The system was efficient, and worked on a time switch. All I had to do was remember to order the gas when the indicator showed red.

Gas is delivered by Andrew. He always stays for a cup of tea and a jam sandwich, and I get quite upset when I occasionally find that I have run out of his favorite blackcurrant. He is very helpful and hard-working. At his suggestion, a couple of years ago, I changed the little box on the wall for a bigger, newer, and better model. This too works on a time switch, but you can over-ride it and put the heating on and off as you like. You can also flick another switch and use it to heat water only, and not radiators, in the summer. I can't fault it. It really is "happy ever after."

When I look back on all this, I can laugh, but it wasn't funny at the time. As a final joke, I was dealt an ace on the day the bigger box was fitted. (The box is properly called a boiler.)

Andrew's boss came to do the job, and I wondered why he kept going in and out to look in his van. Eventually I asked if he had got his dog in there.

"No," he said. "It's my youngest. My wife wanted to go out for the day, so I've had to bring him with me."

I wish it had been a spaniel. I could have coped easily with that. But I did my best, for of course I had to tell him to bring the toddler in. We watered all the plants in the garden about five times. We fed Harold four times. We went up the riverbank and fed the ducks. We went to see the goat. We picked up all the leaves in the pub car park and poked them down the drain. That is, the toddler did while I kept glancing apprehensively at the windows to see if anyone was looking. I got a headache, I felt exhausted, the day was forty-eight hours long. I am not at my best or ablest with the very young. They have so much free-range energy, and they talk – on and on and on.

When I rang up to order some gas the other day, Dad answered the phone.

"Oh, hello," he said. "Still pleased with your new boiler?"

"Yes," I said," delighted. Ask Andrew to bring me two more gas bottles next week, will you?"

"Sure. Next time I'm round your way on a weekend, I must bring my nipper in to see you again."

"Oh, do," I answered, faint with horror.

I shall really faint if he does!

# Winter Morning

The sky is black velvet. The stars, in all their glittering glory, are brilliant. Overhead is Orion, a constellation so easily recognized with his sword dangling from his belt. The air is clean and fresh, and mild for mid-winter. In the wood an owl still calls, his cry mingling with the first notes from the robin. Distantly, I can hear rooks, perhaps early risers from the rookery three miles up the valley.

In the bare bushes I can just discern a tiny shape flitting from twig to twig. It alights on a high branch of the viburnum, whose sprigs are covered with small pink clusters of sweetly scented flowers.

Now, from this tiny creature there comes such a song, such a volume of sound, that it seems impossible for so small a body to have produced it. But I can see her silhouetted against a faintly lightening eastern sky, and the tiny beak is wide open. Her wings quiver with the intensity of her effort, and the ripples and cascades shower the still air with sweet, untutored grace. Her little tail is cocked up at that comic angle which clearly indicates a wren.

Standing there in the garden, still as a statue, I watch her. The tiny throat is vibrating, her head thrown back, her song telling of I know not what. But of this I feel sure; she sings not from aggression or territorial claim, but from joy. Alone, she has come through her night once more, safe from any predator, ready to go in search of another day's sustenance, to warm her, and keep her fit to survive the rigours of cold which may yet come. I am humbled, as I stand and listen.

Alone, she sings, and the sky behind her now glows with a golden light, tinged with rose at the horizon. Joy quivers in her song and hangs on the air like incense. She seems to tell her gratitude for the new day. The stars have paled and gone...and suddenly, so too has she.

I may never share such a moment again with that little singer. It chanced that I was there while she – or he – was there, and my day is the richer for it. Other birds have come now, clustering round the bird table, and the colours have returned to the garden. Red stems glow like rubies in the rosy light. The golden leaves of a shrub light up and reflect the gold in the sky overhead, which is flushed like a ripe apricot as the sun lifts clear of the horizon.

Soon, I know, all this radiance will fade into another winter sky of pearly grey cloud. But I have been given a memory which will light up my day and every day, whenever I look back and recall that little singer in the dawn.

# Spring

February, March, April...these are my months of spring. The days "give out" a little, the snowdrops and crocus march in a growing army across the waking garden, the birds' dawn chorus begins to swell from a trickle to a flood, Hedgehog will wake, and the swallows will come back to the village. I am torn in two. I want it all to happen slowly, and yet I am impatient for the delights of my favourite season.

The French have a legend that on Valentine's Day the birds choose their mates. Perhaps that is why the sparrow fights in my garden now begin to rage more furiously – the row they create is amazing. They make me think of rough inhabitants of a block of flats, where a squabble between neighbors soon spreads into a free-for-all. They have a zest for life that makes them among the liveliest of bird-groups in the garden, always noisy, always in a gang, always busy.

In February we once had three freak days of summer. A heat haze shimmered over the moors, and all the sheep sought the shade of the leafless hedges. Then we went back to winter, and the end of that week saw storms of sleet. All the celandines, which had opened yellow stars, shrank down again, and all those who had seen us go out in blouses and shirt sleeves, warning, "We shall pay for this", now nodded their heads wisely.

There was another year when the spring was mild, and the hedges came early into leaf. Then a vicious east wind blew for three days and burnt the green into brown shreds. It took weeks for things to recover. But that is how spring advances, tentatively, with here a step forward in a westerly breeze and a warm spell, and then a retreat at the harsh bite of frost.

Pots and tubs of vulnerable plants yo-yo in and out of my conservatory when frost is forecast, and overflow into the kitchen if necessary.

There are broad beans coming along in their cream cartons, and peas looking splendid in their plastic guttering, both in the conservatory. The guttering idea came from a TV programme, and I find it very useful for bringing peas on early, where mice can't steal them. All you do is fill manageable lengths of plastic guttering with good compost and plant your early peas there. End-stops prevent things from sliding out, and I find that a sheet of plastic over the top keeps things moist and warm until the shoots are well up.

Meanwhile, you have prepared a site for them and cloched it to warm the soil. When the peas are two or three inches high, you harden them off a bit by day, and then, well-watered, you slide them out into the waiting shallow drill. (Choose a mild spell for it.) In go the first twiggy pea sticks, back go the cloches, and the peas will soon romp away. If frosts threaten, a bit of straw, leaves, or earth drawn up the sides of the cloches will protect them, and in April you can gradually harden them off properly, and will be picking your first peas in early June. It's no trouble in practice, and not only protects from mice but stops birds pecking the young plants too. It is safe to use slug bait under the cloches as, with end pieces, no animal can get in and eat it by mistake.

This is the only time of year when the garden looks weed-free. I feel that at last I have conquered them, when I look at the clean earth on an early spring day; then the mint starts poking through where it shouldn't, nettles creep out from the hedge, and horrid bindweed crawls along the border once again. By May, I know that I shall only just be keeping my end up in the battle.

"If you can't beat 'em, join 'em"...so one year I tried cooking nettle tops. Like a tea-picker, I took only the top bits; I cooked them with care, drained them, and put butter on the result. Revolting!

Out and about, I see the work of hedging, ditching, and stone wall repairing going on. There is skill in these routine jobs, and a well-laid hedge, with the branches nearly cut-through so that they can be pulled down horizontally, clearly shows this. Too much, and the sap won't flow and the branch dies; too little and "'Er won't lie proper." Later on, when the leaves come out, the hedge will be thick and stock-proof. Burnt circles in the field alongside show where all the long prunings were piled and burnt in the cold grey days.

Ditching clears away the dead leaves, junk, and mud, drains off the puddles in the road, and clears the drainpipes so that water gurgles through once again. And stonewalling is a beautiful thing to see in the hands of a craftsman.

It looks easy, but certainly isn't. The finished wall must withstand the scrambling of animals (and sometimes of walkers taking a short cut). It must support itself, and not lean. Sometimes there will be a row of posts and wire along the top, sometimes it is finished with stones laid on their sides. The hole is wider at the base than at the top, and a finished length, newly built or cleaned up and repaired has evenly-spaced and graded stones, giving that look of simple "rightness" which amateurs strive to achieve and just miss. When I dug out the bank along one side of the garden, and revealed an old stone wall, I repaired it – quite well, I thought. But when it was finished, the lines made by the rows of stones had up and down wiggles in them, though I'll say this for it – it's still standing firmly.

I don't know whether it is tradition or due to the nature and shape of the stones used, but an Exmoor well is like rows of dark grey books, whilst a Cotswold one is layers of flat yellowy plates.

Our wildflowers are lovely in springs. This is one of the places where primroses still crowd the banks, and bluebells spread their smoke widely before the bracken and grass swamp them. Dog-violets colour the sunny banks, but hereabouts I know of no woods of wild white anemones, or fields of yellow cowslip.

Purple is a true Exmoor colour. It begins with hillsides lit with rhododendrons, goes on to sweeps of foxgloves, then the bell heather, and last of all heather or ling. I took a friend to see some rhododendrons one sunny morning, which completely covered a steep hill from the blue sky to the sea. It was a sight neither of us will forget. Life is like that here, full of glorious natural splendours.

In February, sparrows, who nest early, may be seen rushing about with bits of straw, and fighting over selected lengths of it. Sterlings appear to nest early, too, and before I had the roof done they regularly built under the cottage eaves. The old nest was a messy affair, full of ragged bits of hey end straw, just wedged on to the rough top of the house wall. When it was used, I heard the birds in the early morning, rattling about, and when the eggs hatched I could time the arrival of the parents with food by the outbursts of shrill chirps. I am sorry that the new roof excludes birds.

By March, the rooks are well and truly into nesting affairs. I like the noise of a rookery, so sociable and busy, and the sight of a head poking over the top as a nest sways up there in the breeze. Tradition has it that when rooks build high in the trees it is a sign of good summer. Since they often refurbish old nests, this is a bit doubtful, but when it comes to starting off new ones, there might be a grain of truth in the saying. Creatures are not daft, and who knows what their wild instincts tell them?

As the spring advances, the farmers gear themselves up for lambing. As one of them described it, "'Tis six weeks of 'ell, and then you collapses."

The sheep have been looking large, and walking about in a stately fashion for some time before the first lamb appears. Then you see a white dot in a field and know that it is starting. Some ewes lamb easily, and some have difficult births, and it is knowing when to wait and watch, and when to intervene that marks the expert. Not that anyone can ever really claim to know it all, where nature is concerned, but experience tells, as always.

Eva used to say that Tam thought like a sheep, and he can often tell at a glance when a lamb is in the wrong field, and its mother in another. Paul has been helping him in the last couple of years, and has given me some amusing tales.

Tam has a caravan up in the field where his sheep lamb, and he stays there to tend them. When Paul spent nights up there with him, Tam wanted to know why he was boiling a kettle after they'd eaten.

"To wash up the plates and cups," replied Paul firmly, for it was obvious that Tam's practice was to use the same ones unwashed for the whole of his stay.

As Paul's skill in dealing with the ewes grew, he found himself going to and fro alone in the dark fields, while Tam issued his instructions from under his blankets. Two and three o'clock in the morning are not the most comfortable hours in which to be about; after one round of the animals he returned to the caravan to find a brimming half pint mug awaiting him.

"What's this?" he queried.

"Just a sip of whisky to keep the cold out," replied Tam.

Another night, he came back to the van and thought that Tam had got up and gone outside. Then he noticed that the humped-up blankets were moving.

"Is that you under there?" Paul asked.

"Ar."

"What on earth are you doing?"

"I'm looking for me teeth."

"Well, you mind they don't bite your arse," Paul said, irritable with the cold.

Last year, when I was in the garden, I could see a ewe with a tiny lamb all alone on the side of a track up the hill, in what used to be a larch wood. She had found a narrow ledge, and given birth there. As I watched, the ewe heaved, and something small and yellowy rolled down the slope for a few feet. It was a second lamb, whose introduction to the world could hardly have been more dramatic. Both Survived for a few days, and then I was sad to find one of them dead. Mineral shortage is one of the causes, I'm told. The other one was the stronger twin, which began to thrive once it got all the milk.

The new-born lamb is not a pretty sight, until it has dried off. I'm not sure if the mother licks it clean, as a cat does her kittens. I carried one into a barn, not long ago, where the ewe had been taken as she'd had a difficult labor and was weak. The lamb was long and thin, wet with yellowy fluid, and streaked with blood. But see it next day...clean and white and fluffy looking, with a black head already turning round to survey the world.

They grow so quickly, and soon achieve that stage of frivolous gamboling which is a joy to see. I often sit in the garden and watch them tearing about on the hill in groups of six or seven. When they stop, presumably for a rest, they poke about aimlessly until one gives a jump and sets off again, the gang in hot pursuit. It is exuberance personified, and is, I suspect, the happiest stage of their lives.

(A clergyman in the village shop one morning stood watching three local ladies who were all admiring Gwenny's new baby in his pram.

"Yes," he sighed, "this is the best time of one's life. You get one woman's sole attention, and all the others hanging over you, saying, Isn' the lovely!")

When April comes, my thoughts turn continually to the swallows. Where are they now, I wonder? Already, in those hot sunny lands, they must have been through the stage of excited fluttering's and gatherings. Now the squat villages and dusty roads and tracks will be empty of their flight and song. Somewhere between there and here, in all that space of sky and ocean, they are marvelously questing their way. How do they do it? How do they know which way to come? The promptings of their nature are so mysterious.

There are many theories. Some say that the wind currents and thermals guide them; others believe that they "tune in" to the earth's magnetic field; they follow the ley-lines, which are proven to be traceable. We have not unlocked a fraction of nature's secrets yet: I hope we never will, because Man has a terrible record of misusing the knowledge which he gains.

I found a dead swallow by the beehive last year, and picked it up. It was virtually weightless, and yet that tiny creature had probably flown over three thousand miles to set here. The white front, chestnut throat and face, and dark back still had a sheen on the feathers, and I don't think it had long been dead. There was no sign of injury, but I suppose even birds can have heart failure, or die because they have reached their allotted span. You don't find many lying about, though.

A feeling of awe came over me as I held the bird in my hand. Cold and wet, heat and sun, had beat down on those feathers; it had sustained life and fed its young, catching insects by the gaping action of its dark beak in flight; its curved wings and forked tail had enabled it to fly with speed and grace. Inside that small body had been the energy of life that made it mate and nest, and rear its brood, and from that throat had poured the rippling songs I love.

I hoped it was born in this village, and had come home, as I covered it gently with earth in a corner by the hedge.

The middle of April sees me scanning the sky for our village swallows. I often see my first one flash low in front of me when I am on the moor, but soon the rest will come, and fill the air above the houses with shapes made silvery in the sunlight. Only when they come down and skim across the grass in wet weather can you see the gleam of blue on their backs. They seem to dream as they glide and turn in the air, their flight so effortless looking.

Snowdrop-time, crocus-time, daffodil-time, tulip-time... all happy days of spring, but my happiest of all are those when the swallows come back to the village.

# A Day Out

There are times when I have every sympathy with Mole (of "Wind in the Willows" fame), who threw down his brush and dusters on a fine spring day and said, "Hang spring-cleaning." Off he went on his travels and so, too, occasionally, do I.

My excursions often lead to a flowery destination.

Some years before I bought the cottage there was a short programme on TV which showed a glimpse of a sparkling stream, and banks and wood-lands bursting with snowdrops. The presenter said that this was to cheer us up in those grey days of early spring, but the location was being kept secret. We all know why – hordes of awful people could otherwise have descended upon it, and stripped the flowers, bulbs and all, leaving a trail of fag packets and sweet wrappers in their place. But it was "somewhere in the West country", and great was my delight when I learned where Snowdrop Valley was.

I set off with a friend on a bright but cold February morning. He drove, and I had the map on my knees. After we had twice taken a wrong turning he stopped the car and said that he would navigate. All I had to do was point the thing exactly where he told me to go. Better progress was then made.

There are two ways to travel. One is to set off in more or less the right direction, and look in all the gardens as you go. I know all the interesting plants visible from the road for miles around. I could point out a few places, too, where I have inadvertently mounted a bank in my gardening enthusiasm. I frequently get lost, but in so doing I have discovered isolated spots whose beauty and peace quite made up for the lengthened journey. And in any case, one is in good company, for was it not Confucius himself who declared that it was better to travel hopefully than to arrive?

The trip to Snowdrop Valley belonged to the other method of travel, after the change of roles and seats. A route was penciled in; directions were verified; there was a scheduled half-hour stop for a picnic lunch... but it was worth it. I would never have found the lonely winding valley, hidden in wooded hills, reached only by buried, narrow and twisting lanes. Or if I had, it would have been after such long delays that the daylight would have faded before I arrived.

As it was, it was perfect. The sun shone through the leafless trees and made the bustling stream sparkle. The snowdrops, in their thousands, gleamed with snowy purity in the wintry light. The hedges were thick with them, and all along the waterside the flowers dipped to their own reflections. They were large fine flowers, nourished, perhaps, by years of leafmould, and I have never seen better blooms in cultivation, or a thicker carpet of them. In one place the ground was so sheeted with white that it looked like a snowfall.

We wandered about, entranced in this wonderland, and our only companions were a man and his wife who knelt frequently to the flowers as they photographed them. Another visit, some years later, showed the valley still unspoilt, and long may it continue to be so.

There are many beautiful gardens in Devon open to the public, and I have visited one of them – Knightshayes – three times in the spring. This, surely, must be its finest hour.

I am not going to attempt to take you on a guided tour in these pages; go and see for yourself, and I guarantee that you will bring back pictures in your mind that will stay with you for years. A tree with foliage of such a delectable apricot shade that one felt like taking a spoon and eating it; two blue and mauve flowering trees twined and blooming together in subtle contrast; a cream rhododendron with leaves backed with brown suede; a woodland glade planted with pink bluebells; an enclosed garden of lawn bounded by clipped hedges, with just a silver-leaved pear leaning over a circular pool... these are some of the pictures I brought away with me.

I also brought, from the plant stall, a pretty double white anemone, which was carpeting a wooded corner, and which is now steadily increasing in mine. This is one of the nicest things about garden visiting... a planting, or a design, or an inspired idea, can be adapted in miniature for one's own little estate.

It was at Knightshayes that I first saw variegated honesty, and it stopped me in my tracks. In spring the purple flowers are always bright and attractive, but when they come with leaves of green and cream, instead of nettle-like plain green, then this humble little plant is transformed. I searched the garden centres in vain for seeds of it, and when I located it in a catalogue and wrote to ask, the wretched company replied that they only accepted orders of a minimum value of £6. (I immediately banned them from my future dealings of course.)

Eventually, I wrote to the head gardener at Knishtshayes and asked if I could buy some seeds of this plant which I now desired desperately, feeling that my garden would never be complete without it. Back came a charming letter, saying that if I would forward 50p, the seeds would be mine. And when they came, there was a little note with them, wishing me "Good Luck." So there is another memory of Knightshayes, happily gracing my springtime scene, and I can't think why more people don't grow variegated honesty. It is so elegant.

Next to gardens, the nicest places to visit for a day out are garden centres. The good ones – and there are two within easy reach – now carry a much more interesting range of plants and shrubs and I defy any keen gardener to come away empty handed.

If space is limited, one should really go with a parsimonious friend who takes charge of the purse upon entry. I usually go on my own.

Much quiet amusement can be had during the course of one's browsing. I once got mistaken for an employee at my favourite G.C. It was quite warm and I was in my trousers and a sweater, and I paused by some pots of clematis which the wind had blown over. I straightened them up, and in no time a nice elderly gentleman arrived, and asked if I would select for him a Jackmanii.

"It's a pleasure," I said, and reached him one with some sturdy basal shoots.

"Now, can I leave it as it is, or must I cut the main stem down?" he asked.

"I should be inclined to leave it for this year – you've got some nice growth coming on," I pointed out, and off he went, raising his hat with the beautiful manners of his generation.

"Excuse me."

This was not the manager, about to ask me what the hell I thought I was doing, but a young woman who wanted a climber for a north wall, and would a clematis do, and if so which?

We had a pleasant chat and I was happy to recommend dear old Nelly Moser, which likes my north wall exceedingly

"Thanks so much," she said, preparing to trot off with it. "I must say it's nice to find someone to who actually knows something here. Usually I can only find the young part-time staff, and they don't know a daisy from a daffodil."

When I eventually got to the cash desk with my own purchases, I was greeted with a broad grin from the assistant, who knows me well as a regular customer.

"I've been watching you," she said. "Let us know when you want a regular job!"

There is a pleasant camaraderie among G.C. visitors, and I felt quite flattered that my assistance had been satisfactory. Not like the man at the railway bookstall, to whom I once offered money for my magazine.

"Don't give it to me, madam," he said huffily. "I'm nothing to do with it!"

Gardens which are open for visiting often have plants for sale, and here one can find both rarities and bargains, and usually the quality is excellent. At one, I have bought camellias for a fraction of the G.C. prices.

Talking of camellias, Marwood is a joy to visit in spring, because here there are camellias grown to a huge size under glass, with flowers as big as saucers. Red, white, and pink, they light a chill grey February day with glory, and a walk through the heated green-house under the branches of its great mimose , dusted with yellow powder puffs, is an experience to be treasured.

Outside, there are more camellias, bursting with fat buds and glistening with rude health. I saw the owner there once, and asked him what he gave them to achieve this.

"I don't give them anything," he replied, which confirmed my belief that not all the magic potions in the world will make a plant grow for you if it doesn't want to. If it likes you, it will, if it doesn't it won't. I speak with some feeling, for even the sturdiest Christmas rose, donated by a skilled gardener though it may be, will take one look at me and quietly fade away.

At Marwood you will see thickets of arum lilies sprouting from the pool's edge, Pieris of rare distinction, and snowdrops in named variety, some of them a foot tall. If you are like me, you will still prefer little nivalis, but it is interesting to see Sam Arnott, and Straffen, and others of which one reads.

I have written previously that if you live in the country you must be prepared for heartaches where animals are concerned. Another of my days out was caused by a dog-emergency.

Peggy used to live in the village, where she spent most of her time 'shut up in a shed. I was so pleased when I heard that she had been given to a farmer, to work with the sheep. My pleasure, alas, was short-lived. Peggy was not proving satisfactory as a working dog, and I'm not surprised. Some of these farmers have only one method of "training" a dog – they bawl and shout at it. Peggy had already been turned into a very timid animal by her previous owner, and it was not long before an acquaintance arrived at breakfast time to say that he had heard that Peggy was going to be shot. (But read on – this story has a happy ending.)

I had a list of animal rescue places, so I made haste to ring round in search of a vacancy. When I found one, I flew to collect Peggy, before the farmer could change his mind about letting me have her. I shall never forget her eyes... they were dark with fright, and when she was lifted into the car she sat motionless. In a kind of dumb despair, sweating through her paws.

It was a long way to "Heaven's Gate", through some very pretty country, which I hardly noticed in my anxiety to get things happily sorted out. But what a reception Peggy got! Those kind people at once realised her highly nervous state, and took her into the office, instead of one of the kennels, where they said they would keep her for the first few days so that she could get used to them. They already had a lady in mind, they said, who wanted a dog from them, but in any case they did not anticipate any difficulty in finding her a home, for she was as pretty a dog as one could wish to see.

The last I saw in Peggy's affair was a soft fluffy pink blanket being taken into the office for her to lie on.

I was invited to look around before I left, and saw dogs, cats, ponies, goats, rabbits, and goodness knows who else, all rescued and living, or temporarily staying, in twenty-five acres of rural peace. It was well-named "Heaven's Gate". On the way out I looked into an elaborate enclosure, and found that even pet rats were accommodated. The enclosure reminded me of one which Harry built for the ferrets he bought at the village autumn Sale (because they were in a cruelly small cage, not because he wanted them for rabbit-catching, as had been their previous use.)

When I saw Harry after this visit, and was telling him about it, I put things in a rather unfortunate way.

"Do you know," I said, "they even take in rats? I thought of you when I saw them."

"Oh, did you?" said Harry. "Thanks very much!"

When I had been living here for two years I had occasion to go back to my home town, to visit my bank's head office and sort out an investment muddle. I told myself that I should quite enjoy the trip, that it would be pleasant to see my old haunts again... but the nearer I got to the houses and main roads and traffic, the more my heart sank.

The bank's head office was, of course, in the heart of the city, and when I had parked the car and started to walk I felt as if my senses were being sledge-hammered. The air reeked of patrol; the pavements assaulted my feet; people kept charging past me; the shops were full of garish rubbish; the noise was a meaningless jangle. Inside the bank, the air was overheated and smelt stuffily second-hand. I looked at the office girls in their smart clothes and flawless make-up, and the young men in their natty suits, and I knew that I no longer belonged here. I was a stranger in the place where I had grown up, and lived and worked nearly all my life. In all those years I had never been aware of the things which now offended – the smells, the noise, and the mad rush.

After I had finished at the bank, I came out and heaved a sigh of relief – and not just because matters had been satisfactorily arranged at last. I could now go home. Two years of living where the pace of life was measured in green and growing things, in bud-break to petal fall, in fruit-set to harvest, and where the air was like wine as it came off the moors, had made me a partner in Paradise.

I drove home speedily, stopping only to buy a bottle of wine. Once at the cottage, I prowled round and round the garden, examining minutely every part and plant, and after my third glass of wine on an empty stomach I fancy there were rather more plants at that end of the day than had been there when I left in the morning.

My last visit to a city was when I took a student to Exeter to sit for an exam.

First of all, we got our meeting-point wrong, so we were late in starting off. I had looked up the route, but somehow the map and the real-life situation didn't agree, and we got on to the motorway by mistake. I cannot begin to describe the awfulness of it. Here were the smells, noise and rush, again, only quadrupled, at the very least. And the dust was an added horror, because the motorway was under repair, as they so often are. Clouds of it enveloped us, full of hard gritty bits, and men dressed in Martian outfits glared at us with mad eyes under yellow helmets, as they wielded fiendishly noisy implements. One felt like a lemming, rushing along with the rest of the traffic to meet one's doom.

However, eventually we met Exeter instead.

While the student was at his exam, I enquired how we could avoid the motorway on our way home. They said it was dead easy.

I must turn left, and keep going straight ahead, so I did, and met all the city traffic in the evening rush hour.

Do people really drive through London and stay sane? It took me three days to get over Exeter!

It would be truer to say that scavenging takes up half a day, rather than a whole day out, though if the haul is fruitful I have been known to make several trips to the source. This is My Dump, a place on the edge of the moor where workmen and various people dump their small rubbish. There is a large official dumping place not far away, where one can take old fridges, beds, furniture, and such like, and where there is an attendant on duty who is reported to make a steady unofficial income from the resale of certain items.

My Dump is a private, irregular affair, probably illegal, too, as sometimes the whole lot is cleared away in one fell swoop-by an avenging council lorry? – but it always creeps back again, in dribs and drabs, though you never actually see anyone unloading stuff. Part of my grate came from there, and so did a piece of iron used as a door stop. A small heavy bin, minus a handle, is put to many uses in the garden; the bird bath was an enormous wheel hub; the garden seat has a back made from the discarded remains of another, larger one; some white tiles, and a few terracotta ones rest in my shed, against the day when they might "come in" for something. So does a box of assorted iron latches, bolts, and bits and pieces.

Oh, yes, if one has nothing else on hand, a visit to My Dump can be like a trip to Aladdin's cave, and until I looked around I had no idea quite how many items had been transported from there to here.

Out on the moor there is another spot where some bits of old farm equipment have been left to rust. I had my eye, for a couple of years, on two big iron wheels, which I felt should be residing on my property and I was most upset when, walking that way with my dear dog Rick, I found that one of them had gone. I resolved that the other should be collected at the first opportunity.

Life is never simple. Opportunity – i.e., time – came when I was suffering from a bout of 'flu, to which, in the early spring, I used to be rather prone. 'Flu or not, I must have my wheel. So I set off, well wrapped up against the cold, and armed with a hacksaw to free the wheel from its axle. A buzzard keened overhead, as I sawed, and a few curious sheep loitered for a while, but otherwise there was just me (dripping with perspiration from a temperature), and the mist drifting by.

I hadn't bargained on the wheel being so heavy. Once freed, I rolled it quite easily down the first hill, but heaving it through the stream and up the other side was a different matter, I shoved and struggled, and no doubt swore, and every yard was a painful battle in which my hands were early casualties. When I was nearly back to the car I suddenly realised that it was too big to go in the boot of the mini I then owned, even if I could somehow lift it in. Was I going to have to bowl it all the way down the lanes to the village thereby demonstrating to my neighbors that I had, this time, actually gone quite mad?

I sat down on a bank to think, feeling hot and exhausted, with a head like a balloon and legs of jelly, in the way of 'flu. There was an empty cottage nearby, used for holidays only, and I decided that If I trundled my wheel into its garden, I might persuade a friend and her husband to come up with their van in the week and collect it for me.

The wheel now rests against my cottage wall, derusted and painted black, and very nice it looks too. It was worth all the blisters, and luckily I didn't give myself pneumonia.

*The wheel remains at the back of the cottage*

A visit to the vet is not one of my favourite excursions, even though my vet is one of the kindest and gentlest. I have great confidence in him, so when he moved further away I stayed on his books rather than go to someone nearer home. If I leave the cottage early, by eight o'clock, I can be first in his morning surgery, and hopefully home again with the patient by lunch time.

My last visit took rather longer. The previous evening I had noticed a lump on my cat's face? Thinking I might be a sting, I waited until the next morning, but it was still there, a bit bigger if anything, so off we went.

I wasn't the first at the surgery, so we sat there (me in my usual state of agitation on such occasions) and watched all the other animals in their assorted baskets, boxes, and leads. Yet again, I marvelled at the cleverness of vets. They can't ask the patient where it hurts, or how they feel, and yet they always seem to know what to do to try and put matters right. Furred, feathered, and possibly scaled, they never seem to turn any creature away – but what if someone took in a pet snake?

Don't laugh at the idea – I had some previous neighbors in the village whose son once had just that, and they told me that it used to glide about freely in the house, and drape itself along the bannisters. Seeing the whites of my eyes, they assured me that when it grew impossibly long, they gave it to a zoo, where they occasionally went to pay Hubert a visit.

What, I wonder, would have happened if Hubert had ailed? Would they have coiled him up in a box and taken him to a vet? And would the vet have died of horror on the spot, as I should have done? Probably not, but I should think that newly qualified ones might feel a little apprehensive at first, as to what each box or cage might reveal.

To go back to Sam.

The vet took a sample and said that the lump was an abscess, which was full of pus, and he would have to give him an aesthetic and clean it out.

"Can I have him home tonight?" I asked anxiously, and was told that I could collect him about midday.

Slightly relieved, I left, hating it when I saw Sam carried off. I had about three hours to fill, so I went to a small garden centre nearby. Round and round I walked, without seeing a thing.

Next I went to a supermarket in the town, and had a strong coffee in their restaurant, still as agitated as when I signed the consent form at the vet's. After coffee and some shopping, I went to my favourite G.C.

I confided in the assistant who had practically offered me a job, on that other occasion, and she cheered me up sufficiently to enable me to look around properly. But though I'm sure I bought something, I can't remember what it was.

At midday, I was back to collect a still-tottery Sam, his operation successfully concluded. Instructions received as to after-care, home. I dove into a very small sandwich for a late lunch, and then Sam and I snoozed off our stress. No, a visit to the vet is not my favourite thing.

However enjoyable a day out may prove to be, the best part of it is coming home. When I first had the cottage, this meant opening the door, putting a match to, or stirring up the fire, and boiling the kettle for tea. Now it means first flying round like a mad thing to feed a gang of indignant creatures. ("You're late. We are waiting.") The birds, Harold and his hen, the cat, the dog, the pony, the goat, the hedgehog... and recently, a tame sheep along the river as well. After which, one may put the kettle on with a clear conscience.

This chapter began with Mole so it shall end with him. How dearly he loved his home, and how perfectly this "special value of some such anchorage in one's existence" is conveyed to us by his creator's pen. Mole looked at all his small possessions in the lamplight, upon homecoming, and told how each was gained, or found, or acquired – how "this was planned, and how that was thought out, and how this was got through a windfall from an aunt, and that was a wonderful find and a bargain, and this other thing was bought out of laborious savings and a certain amount of 'going without'."

Now, that is my idea of a home and a homecoming. None of my aunts ever came forth with a windfall, except indirectly in the shape of two old dining chairs via my mother, but as I look around after a day out, I too am full of contentment to return and be amongst all my treasures again.

# Scraggled's Story

I have just mentioned my tame sheep along the river, so here is her story.

Two years ago, when I took Beauty and Bobbie their daily breakfast, I became an object of interest to several sheep from time to time. They roam freely in the fields and woods, their owners identified by the different initials or colours stamped on their fleeces. One of these always attempted to get her head into the ponies' buckets, so to draw her off, I began to tip her out a bit on the side of the path.

Her fleece was hanging in shreds, and she looked quite an old animal. I christened her Scraggledy, and soon she was waiting for me every morning, and after a while she was ready to eat out of my hand. In the early spring she brought a friend with her, so I was feeding both of them. Then Nature took her course, and both ladies produced a lamb – so then there were four. (Shades of the guineapig era:)

Sheep are moved around from time to time in the course of their management. When they are lambing, flocks of them are gathered into the fields; they are rounded up for shearing, and dipping; they are moved out on to the moors for grazing, and when bad weather threatens in winter, and the snow comes, you will see them folded in the valley fields. There is a pattern to it, though to inexperienced eyes it all seems a bit haphazard.

The inexperienced eyes of a holiday maker once led to an amusing incident. There is a hillside not far away which catches all the sun, and the farmer had a thriving flock on it one spring. The lambs, too young at the time for gambolling and racing about, revelled in the warmth of the sun and the green, soft grass, and lay strewn about in motionless sleep, while the ewes grazed around them. The holiday maker took one look and hurried to find the farmer.

I would have loved to see old Jack Sturge's face when he was told that all his lambs had died!

Scraggledy's lamb wasn't very big when she disappeared. I hoped that she had only been rounded up and pastured elsewhere, but I missed her. I had made a relationship with her, and when you do that with a farm animal, you are always afraid of the worst, of which, as a non-meat-eater, I tried not to think.

In the early part of this year in which I write, the sheep were again in the woods along the river, and one of them stood about on the bank watching me for a couple of days. Beauty and Bobbie had been moved to the lower field, otherwise I would have realised at once that Scraggledy was back, because she would have come for food.

She looked so different – in much better condition, with a good fleece, although she had developed a limp. This was due to part of one hoof having grown out into a long curve, but other than this, Scraggledy was fine, and quickly grew so tame that she came at a call, and ate fearlessly from my hands while I stroked her head. I felt relieved and happy to see her again, and threads of ideas as to her future began to drift across my mind.

She now has her own bag of soaked sugar beet every morning, to eat while I go on my way to the ponies. On the way back I give her some "sweeties", which are pony nuts. At teatime I take her something for her tea, and she runs down through the woods, answering me with eager calls.

Once or twice, when I was late, I had to climb up through the trees to look for her. One afternoon she was in a little pasture up there with a small flock, and it brought a lump to my throat to see her lift her head and come running with her lamb when I called, while all the others sped away in the opposite direction. We had become buddies.

She was only missing for a day when this year's lamb was born, somewhere in the woods. I wondered what her attitude would be towards me now, but when I saw her half-way up amongst the trees, and climbed up with her food, she was unperturbed, and the lamb wobbled round her to have a cautious look at me. I sat up there for several mornings with the warm sun filtering down through the tender green of young beech leaves, the air full of birdsong. Patch and the lamb lay on one side of me, and Scraggledy ate her breakfast on the other.

Now, they both come down to our usual meeting place, and Scragglay allows me to scratch Lamb's ears and chin, which he greatly likes. He also likes playing with Patch, now that he is getting to be a sturdy chap, and one of the sweetest sights I've seen is Patch washing his ears for him, and then both of them having a chase along the bank. Scraggledy isn't too keen on the chasing and is inclined to see Patch off, but it is the lamb who begs for a game. He stands in front of the dog, and does jumps in mid-air, which amazes Patch – her ears shoot up and down –and then he puts his head down and gently butts her, and off they fly.

We have been joined by a very persistent and knowing ewe, who has a brown face, a milk-coffee fleece, and thin, elegant brown legs, with which she stamps upon arrival. Often I have my back turned to the stile and don't see her, but the loud thumps always tell me that Stamping Sid has arrived. I thought, at first that she was a ram, hence the masculine name.

In fact, the more you get to know the sheep, the more you realise that they have their differences of character, and you distinguish one from another more and more easily. Sid stands out because of her colour, as well as her stamping, and so does a ram with long grey and white hairs blowing about his face and a rakish red tag on one of his ears. His eyes are pale and wild-looking, and he charges about, so, falling into the local tongue, I refer to him as The Mad Bugger.

These differences of character make it all the more hard to accept the traffic in animals for food. They would almost all relate to us, if they could, and I hate to see the roughness that goes on in the handling of them. When the sheep are herded you can hear the distress in their cries, and their fear of all the shouts, whistles, and barking that goes on. Animals are not just things.

I said that ideas as to Scraggledy's future were beginning to drift across my mind. If the farmer will sell her to me, would an animal rescue centre take her? And if so, would it be fair to move her away, and restrain her, after she has roamed freely? Ideally, I would buy her, and have her marked in a distinguishing way, and she would stay for the rest of her life in her known environment. But would it work? I don't mind being labelled a sentimental fool – but could one trust others to honour the agreement?

Meanwhile, it is now time to take the dog for her walk, and give Scraggledy her tea, with a bit on the side for Sid. I hope I shall be able to write a happy ending to her story, in due course. Otherwise, the echo of her call, the warm thrust of her questing nose, and her calm, trusting gaze, will haunt me forever.

# Communication

A few miles away from the cottage is something I look forward to seeing every spring. On a patch of moorland, high above an expanse of country which unfolds and rolls to the Quantocks, with a glimpse of the far Mendips in the grey-blue distance, there stand two slanting stones.

Their precise origin is unclear. They may be boundary stones of the ancient Exmoor Forest, for they are mentioned as Fifestanes or Fifstane in the perambulations of the boundaries in the 13th and 14th centuries. But they may go back much further than that, and be the remains of some prehistoric stone circle or row. Here, every spring, I look out for two flourishing clumps of yellow daffodils planted at their feet.

It gives me a little shiver of pleasure to see them. Someone, in planting them, has looked back over the ages and thought of other men who once lived and moved and had their being here. The common humanity in each has bridged the mists of time; those men of old knew pain, hunger, pleasure, fear, desire, just as did whoever planted the daffodils. It is as if a hand, stretching out across the vast gap in the centuries, has touched for a moment those other hands of long, long ago.

Enough is known to trace the development of early man and his whereabouts in North Devon. The acid soil destroys bones, and ploughing has reduced the volume of archaeological finds, but even so, we have our share of hut circles and standing stones and artefacts that speak to us of our ancestors.

Among the many staff who came and went rapidly at the hotel/local pub, under previous owners, was a young man called Alan. He was an archaeology student filling in the long vacation, and he and others liked to call in at the cottage for cups of tea and coffee, and to let off steam when the going was hard. The hotel was not in those days a happy workplace.

One day Alan walked in with a fragment of pottery which he had found on the site of a Roman signalling station not far away. Later on, I went to visit the site and had a good poke about, but could not convince myself that any of the bits chucked outside the numerous rabbit burrows were related to pots. It was an interesting visit, nonetheless.

The site is quite large, ringed with ditches and ramparts, and commands a superb view of the Bristol Channel and the Welsh hills. There are no Roman roads about here, so the station was probably reached and serviced by sea, and a steep climb those chaps would have had. Their supplies were dearly won, carried all that way, first over rough, rocky shore, then up through thick woods, and finally across a windswept height. The purpose of the station was to maintain a look-out across the Channel, particularly for any movement of the wild tribe of the Silures under the chieftain Caractacus (or Caratacus), who was not captured until AD 51.

When I stood up there on a bright sunny day, I tried to picture to myself the Roman garrison as it once was. All I could see was some poor wretch wrapping his cloak round him against the wintry sleet of an Exmoor night. How he must have longed for Italy and the warm south, and cursed the fate that had led him to this god-forsaken spot!

It was a site well-chosen for signalling to the fleet further up the channel, for a good beacon would show from here as clearly as, in reverse, the wartime fires of the blitz showed from Bristol, weather permitting, of course.

The effect of the weather on such a station was clearly brought home to me when the Queen celebrated her silver jubilee.

To round off the day, a chain of beacons was lit across the land, starting, if I remember correctly, with one lit by the Queen herself at Windsor. Dunkery Beacon was to be the signal for the next one across the Channel on the Welsh hills,

That June night the weather was appalling. It blew a gale, and the rain came down in sheets. The clouds were low, and a grey murk obscured all. I went up to a viewpoint with a few other stalwarts, and though we could see Dunkery bravely flaring, we couldn't see an answering glow from Wales. I was soaked after only a brief sortie from the car, and full of admiration for a little group who had obviously come with the intention of making an "occasion". They sang "Rose of England" in the pouring rain; the wind tore the sound from their lips, and we could hardly see them in the gloom. Those Roman eyes would have had to keep a very sharp look-out indeed, as they tried to pass signals up the Channel to the ships. How did they keep their timber dry enough to burn fiercely and well, I wonder? For this is "Glorious Devon", where it rains six days out of seven!

Thinking about communications has reminded me of how aware I have become of the birdcalls. In a small garden where they are constantly and regularly fed you gradually recognise "your" birds, and learn their calls. A pair of blackbirds Mr. and Mrs. Quip have been frequent visitors for three or four years; they mate for life, and I know this pair well. A sustained series of sharp "pink-pinks" tells me that they are agitated about a cat somewhere near their nest; a rattle of sharp notes means that something has frightened them; when they are waiting for food I get a gentle reminder in the form of soft "quip" sounds; night and morning, and sometimes in a pause in the busy round of feeding young, I hear Mr. Q's song floating down from a telegraph pole, where he likes to perch. As sweet as the pipes of Pan his tune rings out, and can do nothing else but down tools and make a pause in one's own busy day to listen to him.

I was most amused one spring evening to see a neighbor's cat, which had obviously been after the nest, fleeing in terror with one of them chittering angrily a foot behind him, flying almost at ground level. The cat got the message, and I never saw him in that corner again.

When I am working in the garden, usually doing something urgent in the sowing-thinning-transplanting line, I quite often become aware of the persistent crying of a lamb. Some note of urgency tells me that this one is in trouble, and then the Private Lamb Rescue Service goes into operation. I climb the hill just across the field at the bottom of the garden, and usually find that a lamb has squeezed under the pig wire which fences their field, and dropped down the bank, from where it can't get back up. If it is very little I can easily catch it and lift it back to Mother. When they are bigger I have to try and head them into a corner or a thick bramble bush before I can get hold of them. When they have small horns, they often poke their heads through the square spaces in the pig wire (because of course the grass is always greener on the other side), and then they get hooked in it when they try to pull their heads back against. It is an easy matter to push their heads down and free the horns, but other Lamb recuses can take some time, during which I think testily of my interrupted job. But when I at last catch the wriggling body, with wool of a surprisingly stiff springiness, and restore it to Mother, and hear the contented bleats as it resorts to the milk bar, I know that it is worth it.

Climbing the hill on Lamb rescues certainly stretches one's legs, and a good pair of the same is vital to the enjoyment of Exmoor, as climbing the slopes of the combes is mountaineering in miniature. In times past, necessary travel was only by means of legs, horseback, or, later, a seat on a farm or carrier's cart. Long strings of pack horses were a familiar sight; the village still has a packhorse bridge, no longer usable, close to the wide newer one. Farmers used it to take their corn to the village mill on ponyback. You can still see the old grindstones, set ornamentally into a stone wall on the site of the mill.

Wheeled traffic depended on good roads, and carts and wagons were probably still uncommon here till late in the 18th century. It was not until the famous John Knight came to Exmoor and began to remake the old roads, from About 1824, and built new ones to replace the existing rough tracks, that communications with the outside world became easier. In my time I have seen the Lynton to Porlock road widened, amongst others, and one of the stony tracks out of the valley converted to a proper road.

I have also seen the change from a local postal delivery made on foot to the red mail van round. Dear old Mr. Rickerts, whose blue eyes always had a twinkle, made his round in all winds and weathers with the true walker's steady, even stride. He never hurried, but he covered long distances amazingly quickly.

Our postmen today are a nice group of men, who will obligingly pass on verbal messages through the valley and even drop-off an urgently requested item from a shop. Imagine that in a town! Their union would probably have a fit, or a strike. In snowy weather I have known them liaise with the local police, who wished to be assured that the sole occupant of a lonely house was alive and well.

The scattered nature of North Devon farms and the isolation of its hamlets and villages all helped to keep its feeling of "difference", especially round about my village, and others near the steep coastal inclines. One-in-four hills used to be as good as a defense system.

It was the 19th century that saw the greatest change, with the coming of the railways. There was a local branch line from 1898 to 1935, but a coach and horses still ran from Minehead over Countisbury to Lynton even in 1920. The one-in-four hills were negotiated with four regular horses, and two extra on the gradients, with a change midway at stables which no longer exist. This was no mean feat when you realise that in addition to the heavy coach there could be half a ton of luggage on board. But the railway meant that journeys could now be made for pleasure instead of only from necessity, and the tourist industry was born.

And then came the cars...

Well, I was glad enough of mine to enable me to get here at weekends, and a shopping jaunt twenty miles away is pleasant enough out of season. From Whitsun until early October the influx of cars is a nuisance which one tries to endure patiently. Tourism brings money into the local economy, and since the mechanization of farming, with the consequent drop in manpower needed, the BandB trade has provided a welcome source of income.

If only they wouldn't leave their litter behind at picnic spots! If only they would practice on hills before coming here with their caravans! And also, if only they would practice reversing! A five-mile journey along the valley can be quite time consuming in the season, as some of the drivers appear to be novices with their reverse gears. They wobble about, or mount the banks, and look either terrified or furious at what one of us locals is cruelly obliging them to do.

Much fun and games occurs when the unfortunate motorist meets Tam in one of his cars. I don't know his source of supply, but Tam has a succession of cars which rarely last him longer than a year. No matter what they are like when he gets them, they soon have flapping mud guards doors tied up with string, missing windows, and often a sheep bawling on the back seat. The horrified motorist takes one look and backs away as rapidly as possible from Tam's battle-scarred wreck. He just sits there complacently, with all the time in the world to watch the queue building up on both sides of him.

Sometimes he has a flock sheep with him, which in the local manner he is herding in front this car. I have seen one of these rear up in the melee and thrust its head and front legs into a driver's window, and the ensuing flow of Language was quite creative.

However, on the whole good tempers prevail, and the only real problem in our narrow lanes is when the fire engine or ambulance has to get through in a hurry. Fortunately this isn't often; our local doctor has solved his problem by resorting to a motor-bike at the start of the seasons.

Before TV, with its live news coverage, the arrival of a morning newspaper on the doorstep was an important start to most people's day. We have several local newspapers, one of which – my favourite – has been going since 1860. Think of that – Victoria was only 40 years old, and Prince Albert was still alive; Gladstone, Palmerston, and Disraeli were directing the course of our history. Now we also have a very local newssheet which is distributed free in the area.

This one should have samples preserved for posterity. It is full of the nitty gritty of daily life as it is really lived here. Births and deaths are recorded, with thanks to the local doctors who provided the care. A fortieth birthday is cheekily advertised on someone's behalf. The whereabouts of a lost pet is sadly sought. Someone else is selling an unwanted wedding present (and what lies behind that ad?) Another is anxious to buy a dolls' house. Church fetes, coffee mornings, car boot sales, cricket and football fixtures, flower arranging demonstrations, sponsored walks, crime prevention, the Mayor's letter – it is all in the newssheet, and makes riveting reading that a future historian would give his eye-teeth to get hold of.

The village also has a parish council notice board. I often see visitors studying it, but I always forget to look.

People think I am mad not to have the phone in. "However do you keep in touch?" they ask. "By the grape vine," I reply, and it's true.

I have been invited to a house-warming party, via the local AA man asked by the organizer if I would prefer to do teas or go on a stall, via a neighbor. Likewise to a sherry party. I have been invited to go and pick mushrooms in someone's field, via the village shop (accepted with alacrity.) News of a death travels swifter than any, and also bad news. "Your goat's got out" can be the unwelcome sequel to a knock on the door. I don't need the telephone?

To keep in touch with friends further afield there is the pleasure of letters sent and received. Most days the postman brings me something even if only a catalogue. In autumn and spring I get a spate of garden ones, and chores are apt to be interrupted when these arrive. At Christmas and Easter there are cards, and I get quite a lot of picture postcards from all over the place during the holiday season, which remind me that there is still a world out there. Of all the modern forms of communication I think I should miss the postal service most.

The Village post office is now only open part-time. I can never go in without taking a biscuit for my dog friend, Romeo. He has the most flirtatious eyes I have ever seen in a dog, and we have long, sloppy conversations over the counter, after he has dealt with the most important matter – his biscuit. He won't eat his breakfast until I have made my regular Tuesday morning call.

What a change the coming of the "Wireless" must have made to lonely and rather cut-off places such as this once was. Suddenly there was London in your ears with Big Ben through the crackles.

Remember all the tuning that went on to eradicate the whistles and squeaks? But what a joy to a lonely woman in an isolated farmhouse, as she toiled through the unending battles against dust and mud and feeding hungry men and children.

So I thought! But one local man said to me, "We're always a bit behind the times down here, you know." His father didn't buy a radio until 1940, and this was a battery set. The batteries were charged at what is now a guest house, where there was a 110-volt dynamo, which also supplied the village with electricity. (Mains electricity didn’t arrive until 1964-5. To the farmers, radio was "new-fangled", and they didn't bother with it. So much for my imagined picture of the farmer's wife enjoying music while she worked!

It was also pointed out to me that a radio was a luxury in those days. Sheep subsidies didn't come in until 1941, with others in 1943 to encourage more food production; guaranteed prices for farm produce came in 1947, followed by grants for the improvement of hill farms, and then better times hastened the modernisation of farmhouses and cottages. Now you would be hard put to find one without that other one-time luxury – a television.

When I bought the cottage it boasted the biggest TV aerial in the whole village. It was fixed to the old chimney, and I was in constant dread of a gale bringing both crashing to the ground.

The problem was solved for me in 1976, when the BBC changed its transmissions from 405 to 625 lines. This piece of technical information means absolutely nothing to me, but what it meant to the village was that in our situation we should no longer be able to get TV. Consternation all round.

One evening there was a public meeting at the village hall, when a spokesman from the Beeb came and told us that whereas the new aerial that was going up on the headland would beam the signal in one direction, it wouldn't wiggle it down into the valley for us. Neither was there going to be any help in the matter from the Beeb. We were advised that the only solution was to get together and install our own aerial and cable system. The name of a competent local engineer was mentioned, and that was that.

The next thing that happened was a meeting in the village pub, organised by Den and a newcomer to the village, who was nevertheless – local Big Joe. They had been in touch with the engineer, who was willing to come and do a survey, so what was needed was a show of hands to see how many people were interested. About fifteen were keen, so it was decided to go ahead. We knew that the scheme was possible, because Henry and John already had their own aerial and cable to their house, and to the one they owned in the village.

The survey done, and a cost arrived at, another meeting took place at which a committee was formed. We agreed to make our firm commitments by a certain date, and here I must pay tribute to the efforts of Den and Big Joe. The more who joined, the less our individual contributions would be, and the cost of running the scheme, and these two foot-slogged around the village to persuade the waverers.

If this all sounds very matey and co-operative, it was far from the case. You have no idea of the difficulties that came to light, and the feuding that went on. B. would not allow A. to have their bit of cable over his property. C. would not agree to the system's cable running under his field, so there had to be a detour. Those who were willing to help dig out the line of the cable would pay less than those who didn't, and there was a squabble when two or three dug the lot and pocketed the "digging money". X. sat on the fence and wouldn't join until he saw that the system worked, and then was up in arms because he was charged a lot more than anybody else.

So it went on, but at last we had our system, and it worked perfectly, with the added bonus that whereas before only a black and white picture was obtainable, now everyone could have colour. Den went out and bought an enormous colour TV on the morning of the great switch-on, and stayed in all the rest of the weekend, watching. Eva and I were the only two people involved who kept their black and white sets – and mine's still going!

In spite of the troubles, our system-which was, I believe, the first one in the country – is well-run. We have a proper association, with audited accounts, an AGM, a committee, insurance, and a set of rules vetted by a solicitor. Since its start, a few more people have joined as properties have changed hands, and now there are nineteen of us.

When you stand on the hill and look down on the Village it all looks very peaceful. But we still have our little local difficulties. One of these is getting people to declare the existence of second points for TV in their houses, for which they should pay £10 per year extra to the annual subscription. This, at present, is £25, and really very low. But you try collecting it in on time!

Once, the committee cut someone off for fiddling with the system and putting in his own undeclared second point. Several households are suspected of having them, for which nothing is paid, because it is an easy enough DIY job to put in another point. A previous chairman was voted off the committee because all the evidence pointed to the fact that it was he who had tampered with the aerial. Another member had to be cut off for non-payment of the sub. Someone else, on the verge of the same action, paid his at five minutes to midnight on the last day of grace! And a cable was broken off deliberately because of a feud that was going on between two people.

Yes, it goes on. Now there are only five of the original members of the association left, and it is becoming more difficult to keep a committee going. It would save a lot of future problems if the Beeb would do something else even more technical, and restore our village, and others like us, to the normal system.

I might even buy a colour TV to celebrate.

# The Vernacular

It isn't always the big events or serious conversations which stick in one's mind. I find myself still smiling at some of the remembered snippets from the past.

There was, for instance, the single sentence I overheard as I passed two women talking at a front door.

"So, my dear, she had to have her leg baked."

If only I could have lingered, with my ears glued! Why, how, and whose, might then have been clarified, instead of puzzling me for years.

I cherish still the reported question issued to a light-fingered lady, who picked herself a cutting or two from a choice plant over-hanging a garden wall. Up reared an elderly gentleman from behind it.

“Is that in your way, madam?" he enquired sternly.

Our local dialect has a pleasing cadence, and there are still people around whose imperfect schooling leads them to an individual turn of phrase. That is why John urged me not to sow my seeds too early “because you can be a bit too previous here."

Aunt Maud, whom you have already met in these pages, would roll out her condemnation of some misdemeanour with a fine flourish.

"T'aint right. T'aint proper. 'Tis wicked!”

I must admit that the most favoured adjective locally is bloody, and most of the locals cheerfully refer to each other as buggers. Yet it isn't meant to be, and doesn't sound, offensive. Neither was one person's nickname, for it referred to her own oft-repeated word. She was known as Pissing Phyllis. And when someone refers to Fat-arse, we all know to which, (but respected) local lady this applies.

One year, I decided to make some Christmas puddings early in the autumn. I used an old, good recipe, but made rather more than I intended, and ran out of pudding cloths when it came to boiling time.

"I've solved the problem," I eventually told a friend who had been here for lunch.

"What did you do?"

"I used some men's handkerchiefs."

"WHAT?"

"They were clean new ones."

"Thank God for that" he said fervently.

Speaking of Christmassy things, I still like to recall the message which I was asked by the then-incumbent of the little local church to deliver. He was a Northcountryman with a broad accent.

"Tell Bob," he instructed me, "that: 'ees ter coom and sing 'is cards."

This same church urgently needed funds for the restoration of its tower. One of the tiny regular congregation, although a relative new-comer to the area, did Trojan work in publicising the need, and achieved a mention of it in the national press. Soon afterwards, she and her husband were most amused when she received at her home a postal contribution addressed to St, Mary the Virgin.

My garden contains a treasured and unusual shrub, which is called stransvaesia davidiana palette. When I saw it in a garden centre, my feet skidded to a halt. Its evergreen leaves had the most beautiful variagation in shades of green, cream, white, and copper, and the copper tints positively glowed on that sunny day. I was with my deputy, who wished to buy a stone ornament as a permanent memento for his colleagues, and we had just chosen it. (He was retiring.)

"And I'm going to buy this shrub for you," he said, ever the soul of generosity.

I looked at the price tag. "You can't do that," I said, aghast. "Its £8!"

At which he smiled and replied, "What's £8 against eternity?"

I have loved my beautiful shrub ever since.

I once asked my vet if he liked gardening, when he was here at the cottage. He glanced out of the window, shuddered slightly, and said, "My idea of gardening is a ride on lawn mower, and a can of weed killer."

We have a couple in the village who often raise a smile, because she is always telling us, "Poor Mac needs a holiday – he works so hard," whereas we all know that he never makes a journey without a two-hour break in a pub.

The previous landlord of our local could never resist a dig when Mac came in. "How's the car, Mac? I saw that you'd broken down out-side the Dragon again yesterday."

This was always received with frosty silence, as Mac tried not to see the twinkles in our eyes.

Between Lynmouth and Lynton there is a famous cliff railway, which saves a long and very steep climb up the zig-zag path to the top. One day I was walking past the ticket office when I heard the following conversation between two trippers.

"Gladys, do you feel like walking up to look at the shops?"

"No, Vi, that I don't. We'll ride up on the vernacular railway."

I've never called it anything else since then.

A vegetable shop in a local town carries a good selection of potatoes, so one year, when I'd finished my home-growns, I asked a friend to go there and enquire for organically grown ones.

The teenage assistant looked blank. Then she yelled to the rear of the shop, "Marge! There's a bloke here wants orgleeanic potatoes!"

Naturally, I've used that gem of a word ever since.

Sylvia came to tea one day and told me of a friend who had been desperately worried about some problem. "But it's all sorted out now," Sylvia said. "As she said when she rang me, 'the Good Lord never comes early-but He's never late.'"

Dave's old sheep dog slowly drew towards her close of life, when he retired to the village. I saw him standing in his garden early one morning, and asked him how Misty was.

Dave shook his head. "I thought 'it would happen," he said sadly. "Last night, 'er sleeped away."

Silently I shared his anguis – surely one of the sharpest of all life's thorns.

When I was exploring a beautiful country church, not far from here, I came across this touching epitaph, which has haunted my memory ever since.

"This grave's a cradle where an infant lyes,

Rockt fast asleep with deathes sad lullabies."

Phillip Steynings, 1634 age 6m.

We all have small memories, like pearls on a skein, and these are some of mine, along with an overheard remark made by a small child – "oh look – there's a beebeebume in that flower".

# A Week In Passing

"Whatever will you do all day when you retire, in a place like that?"

Yes, well...

I looked back in my diary the other day to check on swallow arrived dates, and what now follows is a typical week of my life here.

On Monday I did my washing early, in the usual way – by hand. I'm not very fond of gadgets so I don't possess a washing machine. A bachelor friend said to me once that he couldn't imagine how I managed without one, so I told him that I was really very modern and used solar power. So I do, and wind power too, and a line full of washing blowing in the wind is a jolly sight. When pegging it on the line I have to leave a gap by the bird table, otherwise the birds "do it" on the clothes.

Prior to this, I had already let the cat, Harold and Mrs. H. out, and provided suitable breakfasts. I had also topped up the bird table with food and nuts. Then I took the dog along the river and fed Harry's two ponies (my boys), and Scraggledy, my tame sheep friend. After my breakfast, I put the goat out, and decided to clean her stable. No matter how nicely I make her a straw bed in the corner, she scrapes it all away and lies on the stones. She also regularly tips her box of goat food all over the place.

The contents of her stable make a good addition to the compost heap, but when bagged it is heavy, so the operation made me puff. I revived over a cup of coffee, which, as it was good weather that day I took into the garden. Then a knock at the door caused Patch to fly in and explode in her usual frenzy of barking.

There stood Susan in distress. Her dog had knocked the top off the wart on his head, which I had been helping her to bathe and dress. Now her son, who is a vet some long distance away, had advised on the phone that she should take Rupert to a local vet, as it wasn't healing. The problem was that Rupert's mate, Rollo, would not stay in the house on his own, so could I possibly accompany her and sit in the back of the car with the two dogs? I never refuse to help with animals, if at all possible, so I said farewell to an afternoon pottering in the garden, and was ready to be collected at two o'clock

They were already leaping to and fro over the empty front seat, so I sat in the middle of the back one and took a firm hold of collars on either side of me. Rupert and Rollo are affectionate dogs and know me quite well. They proceeded to mash my legs with their front paws, to thrust their noses into my face and blow in it, and every time I spoke I had to dodge wet licks. They frequently decided that they would like to change places, so we had a tussle. Susan thought that Rupert would be quiet if he could get up on the shelf by the rear window, so I let him go, and that made it easier for him to drool down the back of my neck. Neither of them were quiet in all the twenty miles we had to go; they kept letting out sudden shrill barks an inch from my ears. In addition, they were moulting.

When I got out of the car I looked like a snowman. Brushing at the hairs only made them stick to my clothes more firmly. I said “got out” of the car, but "fell out" would be more accurate, for these dogs were of the dragging and plunging variety, accompanied by chokings and gaspings.

I was astounded (when I had collected myself enough to think). Susan is so well organised and disciplined in her life that I would have expected her dogs to be trained to a high standard of good behaviour. Perhaps she spoils them and lets them do as they like as a form of self-indulgence.

The vet decided to keep Rupert overnight, and remove the wart. I don't mind admitting that I dreaded the request to do another trip to fetch him home, and I thanked all my lucky stars when Susan said that a friend was coming to stay tomorrow and would accompany her.

"And jolly good luck to her, too, “I muttered when I got home, and started trying to get rid of the hairs. I should have got someone to hoover me.

After feeding the hens, the birds, the ponies, and putting Katie away in her clean stable, I took the dog out. Then I got Hedgehog's dish out of the little house where he or she comes nightly for food, hibernation being over, and returned it washed and full of pet food. Patch had her dinner, and so did I, and after shutting the hen house, and calling Sam in, I retired to the fireside with a mug of coffee and a book.

And that was Monday.

On Tuesdays I clean the kitchen. (Other days it gets a flick and a promise.) Today I hurried because there was a nasty job to be done with my bees.

For some time, since they began to fly and forage after the winter, I had been finding a lot of dead bees outside one of the hives. I was back to two again, because they had swarmed last year and I had collected and hived them. Now something was obviously amiss, I had been advised that the trouble is acarine. There was no hope of saving the bees in the bad hive, so we were going to destroy them and treat the others, which as yet showed very few dead bees. I didn’t like what I had to do, but the little creatures were ill, and going to die in any case.

I blocked up the hive, after placing a petrol-soaked cloth inside it, and in thirty seconds the fumes had killed them. Dreadful-but quick, instead of lingering deaths. In the late afternoon, when the bees in the other hive had stopped flying for the day, a beekeeper put in their treatment for me.

This was a chemical-soaked strip of card which when lit and hung in the hive, would smoulder and produce smoke, harmless to the bees but deadly to the mite which caused the acarine disease. It was good to be able to do something positive and help these wonderful creatures after the sad demise of the other hive.

When I look at a jar of honey, glowing like liquid gold as you hold it up to the light, I think that it is the most poetic food on earth. It is the very essence of the flowers, transformed into a food that man has prized for thousands of years. It has even been found in the tombs of ancient Egypt.

If you ever scrape your skin and get dirt in the wound, put honey on it. This will make the lymph flow, and clean the wound for you. And here is a recipe for a delectable pep-you-up drink to revive you when exhausted, or weak after 'flu. Place a raw egg, the juice of an orange, and a generous spoonful of honey in a glass and beat it all together. Then top it up with a good measure of sweet sherry. Down the hatch – and you will think it worth having the 'flu for my Ambrosia!

And that, with pleasant chats and a shared meal with friends was Tuesday.

*Liz and Patch in the cottage*

Wednesday is my "day off"; no chores, and I hope no callers. Apart from the routine animal rounds, my time is my own, and I look forward to Wednesdays. This week I pottered pleasantly in the garden all the morning, weeding, and planting out broad beans from pots to the open ground, but under protective lemonade bottles. Then, as it was a lovely sunny spring day I took Patch for a walk over the moors in the afternoon. Somehow, now that I live here all the time, I don't have nearly as many walks as when I only came for weekends and holidays.

("Whatever will you do all day... etc.")

The sky was pale, clear blue, and the air carried the fresh, winey tang of the heath. Skylarks rose and hung, rose and hung, higher and higher, their songs a cascade of notes that fell like water drops. There was no-one about, just me and the dog, who spent all her time rustling in the fronds of old bracken. Small blue violets were every-where, and when we dropped down into a combe, the pussy-willows leaned golden heads over the brown stream.

I passed a circular pool where once, on a hot summer day, I had succumbed to temptation, stripped to the skin, and enjoyed an icy dip. Thank goodness the bracken grows tall in the summer-a farmer rode over the brow of the hill not twenty yards away while I was cavorting. I fled into the greenery and held my breath as he descended to the track and passed by, unaware that he had nearly surprised Lorna Doone at her ablutions.

To-day I could see little shoals of fish in the water, darting about and then stopping dead, before darting again. Something went plop from the bank, and made a small vee as it crossed the stream. Further down, a heron got up from his fishing and made a leisurely flight before dropping to a new station. Patch came flying to catch me up and waded into the water, drinking as she went.

Halfway up the side of the combe I could see a green square of turf and a rock outcrop, against which it would be nice to lean and have a breather before finishing the climb and walking back over the moor to the car. It was steep, and I sank down gladly. Something rustled away from almost under my hand as I rested it on the grass. I just caught the flicker of the zigzag pattern on an adder's back. It had been basking in the sun, as I had intended to do.

I removed myself hastily.

Back home, after my animal rounds, I lit the fire as the sunny day gave way to the chill of a spring evening, with a hint of frost to come. The days were "giving out", but the first star already gleamed and glittered, a jewel in the sky; I saw a bat flitter past, and went into my supper with an appetite made sharp by exercise and fresh air.

And that was Wednesday.

On Thursdays, I clean upstairs and polish the brass bits and pieces there. It was only by chance that I found that the window catches were brass, under layers of paint. Sometimes I rue that day, because they are fiddly to clean, but they look so attractive when sparkling in the light. An old house throws up lots of surprises like that. All the doorknobs are brass, too, and emerged unspoilt after careful stripping and cleaning. Perhaps whoever painted them got fed up with the cleaning.

The weather continued fine and warm, so in the afternoon I had another walk, and came upon an animal crisis.

Three or four people were standing on the side of a hill, amongst the short springy heather. When they saw me, they waved and called, and two of them came hurrying down. They had found a deserted lamb, they said, so small that they didn't like to leave it, as they were sure a fox would come and get it. Was I a farmer? In any case, would I come and look?

Up we went, Patch rather surprised to find herself put on the lead, and sure enough, the tiny lamb did look forlorn. It was no bigger than a cat, and there wasn't a sheep in sight. I agreed that it didn't seem right to leave it there all alone. Four pairs of eyes looked at me anxiously.

"We're holiday makers," they explained.

"All right," I said. "I'll see if I can sort it out."

So I picked up the lamb, which engagingly snuggled into my arms for the warmth, and we all walked back to the car. I kept my eyes open, but there were still no sheep around, so I decided to take it home. We all waved, and I drove off with a very curious dog wondering what it was that I had on my lap.

Once home, I wrapped it in a blanket, and put it in a box near the fire while I thought about milk. Eva was alive then; she would know what to do, I knew, so I hurried up the road to see her.

She said that it should have been left where it was! Its mother was probably a Scottie (Scotch black-face sheep), and leaving lambs about is apparently a casual habit of theirs. As it was beginning to get dusk, it was too late to take it back now, so she said that she would ring up Tam, and in the morning he and I could take it back to the spot where it was found.

Slightly deflated, I came home, and was greeted with plaintive little bleats which plainly said, "I'm hungry!"

I had forgotten to ask Eva about its milk, so I thought that it would come to no harm if I gave it warm milk and water. I had a small dropper which I had used when feeding a young kitten once, so I dug it out of my animal SOS box, and set about giving the lamb its supper.

How sweet and tender it was to see that little mouth open, and the busy tongue set to work. It got up on its wobbly legs when the first helping was finished and tried to climb out of the box, so I gave it some more, and yet another refill. Then the dark eyes begin to close, there was a faint, contented hiccup, and, with feet snugly folded, my lamb fell asleep. I felt my eyes fill as I watched it, so small, so helpless, so trusting.

I carried him (he had now become Larry) up to bed with me, put his box by the radiator, and tucked him up for the night.

And that was Thursday.

He didn't make a sound until early next morning, when hungry bleats – stronger ones now – announced that breakfast was wanted. I went through the routine again, and then tucked him up, hoping that he would go back to sleep and I shouldn't have to get up just yet.

Larry had other ideas. He was clearly much stronger this morning and wanting to look about. Out of his box he scrambled, and explored my bedroom. Then he came over to the bed, put his front feet up on the side, and looked at me. His nose twitched and his tiny hooves spread open as he stretched and had a yawn. It was most engaging to watch, and I had to squash firmly the wish that I might keep him. Lambs, like kittens and puppies, grow up, as do all the other small creatures to which we lose our hearts. The sooner I found Tam the better.

We went off in an ancient Land rover, I with the lamb clutched tight in my arms, bouncing and lurching over the track when once we left the road. It was worse than the roughest Channel crossing, except that if he tipped me out at least I shouldn't drown.

As soon as I pointed out the place where Larry was found, Tam said, "Ah, and there's 'is mother, 'tis a yow (ewe), see, and she's come back for 'im."

There were quite a few sheep around, nibbling the young heather, and some of them had lambs. This one that Tam pointed out was standing exactly where Larry had been lying. I handed him over, and Tam carried him across to her, imitating perfectly the cry of a young lamb. She ran to meet him, and when he set Larry down, a quick sniff and a nuzzle satisfied her that this was indeed hers. My last sight of my little guest was his wiggling tail as she stood for him to get at her milk.

"I've learnt a lesson," I told Tam as we bounced our way back to the road.

"Aarr," was all he said.

And that, with belated cleaning-the-sitting-room chores, was Friday.

Saturday is bathroom day, and as I think I have the smallest one in North Devon it doesn't take long to give it all an extra good clean. If I didn't stick to a routine, I should never notice what wanted doing in the house, for I am not a natural housewife.

Someone came to tea one day, and I saw that her eyes were constantly drawn to the curtain pelmets, After she'd gone I looked myself – they were black! So now any hot weather sees me whipping off blankets, mats, curtains, loose-covers – anything washable. The cottage is therefore reasonably wholesome. To quote from the writing on an owl-shaped dish of mine, it is "clean enough to be healthy and dirty enough to be happy!"

Colder weather was now developing, and an overcast sky looked like approaching rain, so I thought I would sort out my wood pile and saw some of it up. This is a lovely job for a chilly day, and log-splitting with a wedge and clump hammer is even better for getting the circulation going. People in the village know that I like burning wood, and anyone who has a good clear-out usually lets me know. I have, at various times, burnt the fittings from the post office kitchen, the rafters from the attics of the village shop, the old window frames and bar fittings from the pub and branches of felled trees from all over the place. It is all grist to my mill.

When my log baskets were filled, and there was a nice pile stacked in waiting, I saw that it was still quite early and I had time to go to the library. This is five miles away, and though I could use the mobile library which comes to the village on Mondays, I prefer to visit the proper one. The other will do for when I am ancient – say about ninety-eight.

I would sooner go hungry than do without books, and Jo, the librarian, ensures that the visit is amusing. She has been married three times, has a lively sense of humour, and knows everyone and most of their tastes.

"You won't like that book," I once heard her tell a small boy. "It's got too many words in it."

To an elderly man choosing books for his wife, she said, "you'll get hell if you take her a thriller. She likes romance".

“I"ll get hell in any case,” he answered gloomily. "The doctor won’t let her get up for another week, and she's livid.”

Then the phone will ring, and it is one of Jo's large family in the midst of a crisis. She takes it all calmly, but her eyes sparkle with a zest for life as she agrees to put up somebody's friend, baby-sit, or possibly look after the dog for a week. I like people like that, although their kind of life would drive me mad.

Back for lunch, I took my colander down the garden and filled it with the makings of a salad. Some sprigs of watercress, growing under a cloche, a few loose sprouts, some Welsh onions, parsley, a leaf each of mint and lovage, both of which were just putting up their new growth, onion and garlic from my store... not a bad home-grown assortment for early spring. I chopped it all up together with scissors, scattered a few walnuts and sultanas over it, and mixed it with an oil and vinegar dressing. Eaten with cheese, or whatever else you fancy, and perhaps a jacket potato, this is the food for pep and health – you can forget about vitamin pills.

Shortly after I had finished lunch there was a knock at the door. I opened it to receive my neighbour with a toad on a shovel. She had found it stuck in a piece of drainpipe, which it must have fallen down inside and been unable to scale because of the smooth sides. Could I please have it in my garden?

We took it up the steps to the grass by the bird bath and gently tipped it off the shovel. Unhurt, it made straight for the vegetation in the border, wriggled under cover, and that was that – another creature rescued and helped on its way. I saw it several times in the garden afterwards, waxing fat and busy – I hope eating some of my hordes of slugs. (I wonder how many other gardeners have found to their cost that 'ground cover' also means slug cover? I am pulling a lot of mine up again.)

Sylvia stayed for a chat and a cup of tea, and we ate the last of some home-made shortcake by the fire, on which my newly sawn logs crackled cheerfully. Then she went home, I saw to all the animals, and walked a little further along the river than usual with the dog because the late afternoon was so inviting.

There is something exciting about the spring, a feel in the air, a tingle in the atmosphere, that speaks of energy and growth and the thrust of new life. I feel as if my hands, placed on a tree trunk, must sense the rising sap within, the life-blood coursing through its veins, that will soon pour itself into bursting buds and shining leaves. Even the moss at its feet has a livelier look as it drinks in the surge of life renewed. There is an urgency of energy all around that must presently spend itself in a crescendo of blossom and birth. I can smell the spring on the wind, and hear it in the increasing volume of birdsong, and I can see it in the catkins that already have shed their pollen and now dangle in long brown tails on the hazel bushes.

And if I stand here much longer, I tell myself, caught up in this miraculous cycle of the earth's life, my feet will take root and my fingers will sprout leaves, and I shall become like Philemon and Baucis in the Greek legend, and be turned into a tree myself.

So, musing, I strolled home again in the first drift of a light rain. And that, with a meal and a book by the fire, was Saturday.

On Sunday mornings I usually drive five miles to church. It is a lovely drive, first over the moor and then down a one-in-four hill from which one has a magnificent panorama of the Bristol Channel and Welsh hills on the other side. It is all too easy to gaze entranced at the changing colours of the sea and sky, at the cloud-shapes and the wheeling white gulls, and find that one has drifted across the road to the wrong side. I'm always doing it because I never get tired of the view. From sea-level, one then goes up another one-in-four hill through woodland, and there cannot be a more beautiful drive to church than this. (And what, by the way, is all this nonsense of signs saying 25% these days? A bit more of daft EEC? I say with Scrooge, "Bah!")

The Norman tower of the church is a landmark; the rest of the building is modern, the result of much restoration and rebuilding, beginning in the nineteenth century, and coinciding with the birth of tourism in the area and the developments that went with it. The result is a beautiful interior. The walls are white, except for one of dark green which sets off the East windows. In the lady chapel an unusual copper-fronted altar glows richly, and the whole atmosphere is warmly welcoming. We are a friendly gathering, on Sundays, and where I sit we are always passing on gardening tips to each other. Some of those present have lived all their lives in the district, which adds to the family feeling. Of all the churches I have ever attended regularly, this one more than any gives me a sense of "belonging."

I am not really at ease with very young children – especially when they yell, or leak, or dribble – but I am always amused at the antics of the incumbent's youngest son. He is at the drunken-toddler stage, and frequently escapes from his mother during the service and sets unsteady course for the chancel steps. On one occasion he collapsed halfway, and began examining the leg of a visitor, who – unused to such goings – on, went bright red and looked round in anguish as his sock was yanked down. On another Sunday, after a particularly mobile session, the toddler flung himself down spreadeagled on the carpet in the aisle with the abandonment of a puppy, and lay there oblivious to the amusement he was causing.

I have reservations about small children in church, but the boys in this family are very well-behaved, if unorthodox. One shot in on a Christmas morning wearing his new Batman outfit. The oldest has recently become an acolyte, and when he graduated to carrying the cross it at first wobbled about alarmingly overhead.

I take my turn in reading the lesson. Sometimes whoever it is forgets, and we all sit there waiting with smug expressions until the Rector steps in. The last time this happened the silence was lengthy. I blush to recall it… for the culprit was I.

I was also remiss in not turning up for two half-hour steward duties when the flower festival was on – I mistook the week. I also got the day of the fete wrong, and arrived at the rectory with a load of home-made cakes on a Saturday.

"Church fete?"" queried the Rector. "We had that last Wednesday."

When I came home from church, on the Sunday of which I speak, there on the doorstep were old colleagues making a flying visit. They had come provided with a picnic, but my freezer always has things in readiness for such occasions, so we set to work, opened a bottle, and lunch was a hilarious if late meal.

How often, on a chilly day, my visitors love to relax by a real fire! I gave Paul the job of keeping it stoked, while Joan and I had a good gossip about mutual acquaintances, and then I left them while I did my animal round. They were both asleep in the glow when I came back.

Tea by the fire revived them for their eighty-six-mile journey home, and I waved them off in an evening already lit with stars, and the gleam of a young moon. How thankful I was to be staying here, when the air was clean, and the only traffic tonight would be no more than a couple of cars and neighbors walking to the pub for a quiet drink.

I closed the door and went to tackle the washing-up, on which had not allowed any time to be wasted. It was six years since I retired, and it gave me a warm glow to be remembered and visited like this.

And that was Sunday. And that was the week, gone so quickly to join all the others whose passing marks the progress of the all-too-fleeting year.

# Blue Poppies

Spring is synonamous with sowing and growing, and this is when I hanker yet again for blue poppies, meconopsis betonicifolia.

I first saw these beautiful flowers growing at Inverewe Gardens in Scotland. A turn in the path brought a woodland corner into view, and I stopped dead. Blue poppies are of the most ravishing sky-blue colour, with a boss of golden stamens lighting the petals. The leaves are primrose-leaf shaped, and not noteworthy, and it is the flowers that hold the eye. Cool, elegant in their simple form, they are so, so lovely.

I'm sorry to go on about them, but they captivated me. I kept going back to look at them.

Off and on, in the following years, I would see tantalizing photographs of them in gardening books. Then one day I heard that a couple living about half a mile away had some growing in their garden I sought out Lady Hold (that was her nickname, she was Mrs. really), and asked if this was true, and if so, might I come and see them when in bloom?

In due time, a message arrived that the poppies were flowering, so I went to look. Sometimes, when one sees again a remembered delight, the impact is not the same. (Who has not met an old flame and wondered what on earth one saw in him?) But here were my charmers, once again enthralling me. The luminous azure flowers floated against a leafy background in a semi-woodland garden, and I vowed there and then – that I would have blue poppies in my gardens Why not? I could provide a peaty, acid soil.

Lady Hold announced that they were soon moving away. The newcomers were nice people, and she would leave a request that in the autumn I should be given a plant of the poppies. Nothing happened – I didn't really expect it to – and of course, I didn't mention it when I met the new arrivals. I did, however, in the following year, ask if they still had the blue poppies.

"Oh, yes," came the reply. "They're lovely. But they were in the way so we moved them."

I gnashed my teeth. Here were people who not only had inherited my coveted flowers, but who casually moved them about as well. It wasn't fair!

Then, when I was at a garden centre, browsing round the seed stand, I suddenly thought of them. Could one get seed? I twirled the rack-and there they were. I could hardly wait to get home and sow them.

How tiny those seeds were! I thought I'd got a dud packet which machine had missed, when I opened it. They were no more than a small pinch of minute specks – a draught would have blown them away.

I think I've had four attempts at growing them, so far. Here are the results.

One: They germinated, and then the green threads of plants sat there unmoving for a week before keeling over. Why?

Two: They germinated, and actually became minute plants with a pair of leaves. I held my breath and pricked them out. Next morning, I swear they'd grown, and so had I, with pride. I took them down to my tomato house, so that they should have plenty of light and warmth under the glass. Two hours later I went to gloat. They were gone! The sun had come out, the temperature had soared, and my poppies had shriveled to threads, which only the closest scrutiny revealed. I thought of suicide.

Three: They germinated. Mindful of the last disaster, I put them on the kitchen windowsill to grow. One morning I came down to find them upside down in the sink, thanks to Sam's midnight walk about. Fortunately for him, he is allowed to get away with murder – even of my blue poppies.

Four: They germinated. I was told that the first lot had probably damped-off, so I watered the compost with Cheshunt compound. They grew; my hopes rose: then, one by one, they got nipped off. Nothing could get in from outside, as they were wrapped in plastic bags. Studying the compost, I spotted tiny grey insects in it, like miniature spiders, and found the culprits.

Just recently, a friend wrote and enclosed a picture of some blue poppies. "How," he enquired wickedly, "are yours?”

I replied that one day visitors would have to fight their way into my garden through thickets of them.

I was therefore delighted, last year, to find that the garden centre which offered me a job had some blue poppy plants for sale. At nearly a fiver each, thickets would have to wait, and I bought one.

No plant was ever better looked after than that one. I repotted it to keep it happy through its first year, and brought it under cover when bitter weather came, and periods of prolonged wet. The hairy leaves seemed unattractive to slugs, and my plant flourished.

Being deciduous, it died down in winter, but when spring returned it put up new shoots – and a bud! Yes, at last, a bud, which steadily grew up into a tall stem with no less than seven flower buds in all. I placed it in a prominent position, so that I could see it from the kitchen window, and drooled over its label, which bore a colored picture of the flower in that delectable shade of blue.

One Sunday morning the hairy calyx split to reveal what I thought was a white lining, similar to that which oriental poppies have.

But alas, that white lining expanded and steadily, before my eyes, became petals. Fragile, delicate, quite pretty, really – but not blue! I am told that in a batch of seeds it is not uncommon to get a rogue white one, and it had been my ill – luck to choose the odd man out.

Not long after, I was in the garden centre, and related my sad tale. As a result, a young man with a most charming voice and manners took it upon himself to send me copious notes on the culture of blue poppies, and he also recommended a recent book on them.

Jo got it for me, at the library, and it proved to be fascinating reading. The French missionary, Delavay, sent a dried specimen of a blue poppy home in 1886; George Forrest collected seed from it in the early 1930's but it was Frank Kingdon Ward who sent home seed which was successfully grown. Before the end of 1925, it was growing at Kew, Wisely, and Edinburgh, and I like to think that the ones I saw at Inverewe were descended from the Edinburgh plants.

From whence came the blue poppies which tantalisingly grow in the garden down the road, I wonder? The house is built in a small combs, and like so many of Exmoor's others, it has a stream of spring water running down through the garden. This no longer gives the house its drinking water, but it, does, give the blue poppies what they love, a moist environment, and a humid atmosphere.

I bought another plant this year from a different source, and I also sowed a last pinch of seed from a packet. Following advice gleaned from the book, one recognizable plantlet and two hangers-on have resulted, so all in all, hope springs eternal!

# Summer

"Summer's lease hath all too short a date..." Yes how right you were, Shakespeare!

Some years, April is still winter; I have helped with hedging on a hillside in this month when the sleet drove straight at you on a knife-edged wind. And when autumn comes early, with twinges of frost in September, or rain and gales that flatten the garden, well, then my summer of May, June and July seems very short indeed. We wait so long for it, and, like the days of our youth, all too soon we are looking back on it.

May is one of my favorite months of all the year. There a can be such radiant mornings, when the young leaves glisten in the sun, and evenings when the sky is a turquoise arch, flung over a world full of birdsong. When there steals on the air the thin, sweet scent of lilac, haunting as the plaintive music of a violin... then I say that Heaven will have to be pretty good to beat this!

In summer the sheep disappear for a few days, to reappear sleek and white after shearing. They have the look of boys whose parents have told the barber to cut it good and short, in the interests of economy.

Crossing the pub car park one evening a few years ago, I noticed a large and woolly sheep unmoving close behind a Land rover. At first I thought it was caught up somehow, but a closer look showed that it was tied on. Something prompted me to wait for the driver, and when he appeared with his pal, they both got straight in and prepared to drive off – with the poor animal about to be dragged and horribly injured behind them. I shot across and asked them if they knew there was a sheep tied on behind?

Mystified, they both got out to look. Then they fell about, laughing.

“I know who bloody did it,” giggled one, untying it and throwing it into the back of the vehicle. "E's give me a lot of trouble, that sheep 'as, when I was shearing today.”

I was furious. I told them off for being rough, and for not caring about what might have happened to it. That caused further amusement, and the remark that it would have had very tired legs, when it got home after running behind all the way.

"Some of you people just don't care how you treat animals,” ‘I stormed.

"Ah, well, I aint always been treated too well myself,” was the answer, and off they went – still laughing.

I was so angry that I went to see Eva, to tell her about it, and she was horrified. She fully agreed that to some animal-handlers, they are just things, money on four legs, and such people are not worthy of the name ‘farmer’.

Now the summer air smells of disinfectant, because the sheep have been dipped. One of the nasties which this removes is tics, which cats, dogs, and humans can also collect. You at first notice a tiny, irritating speck on your skin, which, unless you tweak it off as soon as tweezers can grip it, will grow and swell into a vile blister of your own blood, before falling off. Very nasty. In Africa, this would lead to tic-fever, but here it is just disgusting.

My bird table is as busy as ever in summer, crowded with young sparrows whose gossip fills the air with squeaky chirrups. There is a lessening of bird song, as the months slip by, when the hard-working adults go into their summer moult, before their winter plumage begins to grow.

Katie moults, too, and when I fetch her in at night my clothes are thick with white hairs where she brushes against me. When I empty the hoover bag, I find the shed hairs of Patch and Sam, and I am always brushing them off the cushions and chairs. Once a neighbour called, still in his dark working suit, and before I could stop him he sat down on the settee, where Patch reclines. Alas, it was not a dark suit when he got up to leave.

In early summer, the wisteria covers the rear of the cottage with sweetly scented ropes of mauve. I bought it from a chainstore for £1.25, and for seven years it grew well, but only produced leaves. I decided to take it out, as it was romping too verdantly on its way, and then I relented, and gave it a short back and sides with the shears instead.

The next year it produced thirty flowers; the following one about eighty, and after that they were too numerous to count. Now I keep it in check by the proper, twice-yearly pruning-first in summer to take out unwanted whippy growths and shorten spurs to within five leaves of the base. In February, cold weather permitting, these are cut back to two buds, and then I stand back and wait for the annual treat. I feel very proud of my cottage when I come up the garden and see it clad in its mauve garment. It is, I think, the height of elegance to have a loo window wreathed in wisteria flowers. Later on, the tendrils come right in and visitors make squeamish remarks about the triffids.

Presently you are enjoying the roses once again. I am so glad that "New Dawn" is getting going on the east-facing wall. There was one grown from a cutting on the front of the house where I was born, and its yearly festival of flowers was a sight to see, in spite of its age.

I drove past that house not long ago, and it had been cut down, which was an act of vandalism, in my opinion, so mine is all the more welcome, for memory's sake.

Memory is stirred once again when the white phlox comes into flower, marking high summer. One sniff of their scent, and I am standing in a moonlit garden in the lull between two air raids.

So strange was it to be abroad with one's parents in the small hours, and so beautiful was the scented night, that, even as a young girl, I felt the poignancy of the moment. There might not be a tomorrow... and how piercingly sweet the present felt, beside those gleaming flowers.

This, by Dylan Thomas, often comes to my mind when the first fruits of the garden ripen:

"And down the other air and the blue altered sky

Streamed again a wonder of summer

With apples

Pears and red currents."

The strawberries usually give a good crop; I don't know what variety they are, but their flavour is superb, and the size of the fruits, in their second and third years, is large. Then I start off another lot of plants from runners, on a different site. How delectable are those sun-ripened scarlet fruit! One is mindful of the health warnings about too much fat, but what are strawberries without thick, glorious cream? I cannot help feeling smug as I tuck into mine when Wimbledon is on, and I read that a few measly berries and a dab of what passes for cream costs the earth. For a change, strawberries in fresh orange juice are delicious too – the orange enhances the flavor of the fruit.

Just as the strawberries finish, the blackcurrants are ripe, and unless I am quick, the blackbirds will have gorged the best. I try draping old net curtains over the bushes, and hanging plastic bags on poles nearby, to rustle and swing in the breeze, but the birds are old hands at the game. If all else fails, they get under the bushes and hop their way up through them to get at the fruit.

After this, they remember that the raspberries will be ripening, and move over to the canes. Green netting is draped over the top of them, but they sit on this and poke their beaks through.

They do, however, leave green gooseberries alone. The only way to have your fruit for yourself is to grow it in a fruit cage – but surely one must give a little something in return for all the songs? I agree with Joseph Addison, who wrote, "I value my garden more for being full of black-birds than of cherries, and very frankly give them fruit for their songs."

Well, more or less!

If you want your garden to be a haven for wildlife – and I do – you have to accept losses. In the vegetable garden I have learnt to cloche and cover all my young seeds and plants; once they have grown up a bit, they seem to be less vulnerable. In the flower garden I am gradually replacing the tempting items with those less succulent, but even so, some small creatures nibble out the tender growing tips off quite a lot, and they also eat flower petals. I suspect mice of one kind or another, which live in the garden wall. Earwigs and woodlice are culprits, too. (I have heard woodlice called, by children, by the oddly apt name of 'grandfathers! )

Hellebores and primroses and winter flowering heathers are left alone, and in summer I don't lose aquilegias, Welsh poppies, geranium (the hardy ones), Japanese anemones, roses or cistus, to name a few. In autumn, the flowers of sedum, michaelmas daisies, crocosmia and kaffir lilies remain untouched. I now grow annuals and special plants in pots and tubs, which I can move around, and even take into the conservatory for safety at night, It's a battle of wits!

In the early summer the cottage is suddenly home to ants. I think they live in the old house walls for the rest of the year, but about June they emerge round the kitchen window. After a few weeks they disappear, only to re-emerge upstairs by the landing window. Crowds of them now have wings, so I leave the window open for their exodus. I have also watched them pour out from between paving stones in the garden and take off.

The weather, as always, gives us plenty to talk about. We can never seem to have it quite right – if it's very hot we gardeners beg for rain, and when it's too wet we want sun to bring the flowers on, to ripen our fruit, and discourage the hordes of voracious slugs. Local businesses need a good summer to fill the guest houses and tea shops, and bring the holiday makers to the gift shops.

It is a curious thing, but however fine the weather before and after the day of one local show, the day itself will always be wet. It is almost a tradition. I have seen the lightning snake along the ground on this particular day, the sky seeming to descend to the earth, and last year the wind was so strong that it blew the refreshment tent down. And another strange thing is that whenever some previous neighbors return to the village for a holiday they always bring bad weather.

Good or bad weather appears to build up slowly, with frequent hints of what it intends to do later. Jan was good at foretelling the weather. He told us to expect the long hot summer of 1976, during one of the preceding warm weeks.

“'Tis coming back,” he told me, “and 'tis going to last, I know its.”

And it did, right into mid-October. The grass bordering the beach was bleached to a sandy color, so that the seashore appeared to have widened. Hedges and hedgerow trees died, and Jack Sturge bet the then-landlord of the pub £50 that he wouldn't dare to water the garden with a hose. But he did, and Jack lost his bet, because he didn't know that a standpipe was still giving water from a spring behind the pub, and the hose connected to it was permissible, because the source was outside the imposed restrictions.

Many local people, who are on spring water, had to wait for six or eight weeks after the rains came, before their taps flowed again that year.

Sometimes in the summer my tap water comes out pale brown, although it is from a mains supply. At others it tastes faintly of disinfectant, but on the whole it is good, and visitors remark on its softness.

The less likeable things of summer here are flies, too much traffic, no room to park while shopping, and callers who come to "look you up" while you are doing things up a ladder in the garden. The lovely things are far more numerous. There is sitting in a flower-filled conservatory and watching the birds in the garden; there is drinking coffee outside in the very early morning; there is watching the sun go down over a heat-hazed blue-grey sea; there is looking at the play of young rabbits in the dusk; there is the delight of the long hours of daylight.

The spirit of summer Exmoor is captured for me in a combination of three things... the calls of the sheep, the sound of a stream rippling over its stones, and the sweet smell of early heather in bloom. Now as each day slips by, full of green and growing things, one can hardly remember bare earth in the garden and the first few spears of bulbs. All is lush and ever-flowing from the season's horn of plenty.

# D.I.Y

When I was sorting out the cottage and its improvements, my first bit of DIY was repairing the rendering on the rear wall. Since those days I have progressed to bigger things, with hard labour, modest success, and a lot of satisfaction.

I love DIY superstores. There are three or four within easy reach of the village, and a shopping trip to these gives me a lot of pleasure. Even the local hardware store is an Aladdin's cave of bolts and hinges and screws and useful paraphernalia, with that nice mixed smell of creosote, paraffin and I-don't-know-what pervading it.

As has already been noted, I collect bits of timber. The rear of the garden shed is choc-a-bloc with posts, laths, planks and poles, so that any construction job can often be furnished from home supplies. I also have what I call my glory box, in which is a large store of hook, bolts, knobs, brackets and the like. When the need, the mood, and the urge arise, I can usually get going speedily – for when I get an idea, I am one of those who must embark upon it at once.

I was in my nightly bath when an idea occurred to me about a use for a sideboard, which the amalgamation of furniture from two homes had made redundant in the cottage sitting room. If, I said to myself, hard board were to be fixed over the mirror, and two shelves placed across this, would it not make an attractive dresser for the kitchen? Yes! But would it fit the end wall, which has cupboard doors opening across it from either side?

Still dripping, I hurried downstairs with a tape measure. It would fit, but only if I sacrificed one of the doors for a curtain instead. Up in the attic I was sure that I had a length of curtain material in just the right colour; down in the shed there were several large pieces of hardboard, and timber long enough for shelves. I restrained myself from immediately going to look in both places, but I could hardly wait for the morning so that I could begin.

This proved to be one of those jobs which went like a dream. The sideboard had been in my family for years and my brother and I kept our pens and inks and paints and bits and pieces in it as children. It was solid oak, with carved doors, and it might seem sacrilege to have painted it white, but that is what I did. The paint covered a multitude of deep ink stains, and the white gloss helped to reflect the light at that end of the long kitchen. It is now an often-admired piece of furniture, on which some green china is happily displayed. It suits me, and it suits the cottage, and best of all, the job didn't take long, so my impatience to see results was soon satisfied.

"You're awful-you never throw anything away," I've been told. But even a local builder has been known to call and ask if I happen to have an item needed to complete one of his jobs, and so have the husbands of two neighbors.

The bird table is an essential piece of my garden equipment, and when I made it I had problems in fixing the sloping roof, and the solution came from the greengrocer's. I needed triangular-shaped bits of wood for the roof-ridge, and tomato boxes have corner-pieces of just the right shape. So impatient was I to get the finished table on, its post set up, and open for customers, that I went out and dug the hole for it in pouring rain. One of my neighbours thought I was gardening and called out, "Woman, you're mad!" This bit of DIY brings life and pleasure to the garden all the year round.

I made the hen house out of old cupboard doors and bits of a kitchen unit provided by the pub, as in those days Harold and his ladies resided in their stable, which was underneath a bedroom.

Harold's early morning crowing's were making him very unpopular, so alternative accommodation was urgent. His house still stands, after about ten years, and has survived several dismantlings and movings. I think it will last as long as Harold and his now single remaining lady.

A wood store was easily made for my logs out of posts found on the beach and a left-over bit of larch lap garden fencing for the roof. Sam finds this a very useful spy-post, and this is where I tame the chaffinches to take crumbs from my hand in winter.

The ceiling over the stairs was old original lath and plaster, and every so often a bit of it would fall down. I used to look at cracks in it, and I knew that one day the whole lot was going to descend. I've done small areas of plaster but this would be beyond me, so I wondered if I could put a false ceiling under it instead. The mess which the removal of old plaster makes is amazing, as I know from experience.

The walls surrounding the well-head of the stairs are clad in tongue and groove, and this suggested a false ceiling of hardboard supported at the sides on lengths of four by two laths. (One must, of course, refer to it as four-be-two in the timber yard.) I measured up, wedged my longest step ladder across the stairs, and set-to. I could see that supports across the ceiling would not only hide the joins in the hardboard, but would, if of suitable timber, look like beams. (I smiled as I recalled Valerie and her sharp enquiry, "Have you beams?") No, but I had some pieces of an old draw-leaf table which filled the bill, and when painted black-of course-they looked quite realistic and did the job perfectly. A skilled friend did the wiring to hang an old lantern from one of them, and now the ceiling is secure and decorative.

I am still rather proud of this effort.

Over the years I have learnt to buy good tools, and to look after them; to ensure that wood is always measured and cut accurately, and held by the proper screws. To turn out a neat, sturdy product gives a satisfaction that no hit-or-miss job does, and I have also learnt that good work can't be hurried, and am less impatient for results than I was. (Usually).

The need for accuracy was brought home to me when I made a super for the beehive. It had to sit exactly on the one beneath it, otherwise the next one on top would wobble and the bees would get out through the gaps. It proved to be far more difficult than I expected and my first attempt was all wrong. It wasn't square and it didn't fit. I took it to bits and started again, marking all the measurements more carefully, and this time it turned out satisfactorily – so much so that two beekeepers have expressed surprise that it is home-made.

Four old windowpanes were passed on to me when the pub had some renovations done. They were large and heavy, and I felt that they could be used for something rather special. Glass is always useful in a garden, and I looked at the south facing fence, against which I occasionally tried a few tomatoes. Here was scope for a special bit of DIY!

I cleared the ground, after measuring the windows, and dug trenches to fill with rubble. Then I mixed up some cement-I love cement jobs, so durable and solid-and made a base for a run of breeze blocks. (had a small stock of these, found on my dump, in a corner of the garden.) On them, in due course, I set the window frames, screwed with brackets to a back wall made from an old door. Two pieces, cut to give a sloping support for a roof, were fixed on, and then all I had to do was make the roof from rigid clear plastic and battens, and fix it on with hinges.

In this tomato house I grow Gardeners' Delight every year, and in the winter I use it for lettuce and parsley.

In my cottage there are always books looking for shelves. A friend gave me a cabinet for records some years ago, and I suddenly saw that here was something I am often short of – space. A slim bookcase would stand beautifully on top of it, and could provide three shelves. A base, two sides, and two shelves were all that was needed; two short planks and some bits of tongue and groove furnished my needs, and I spent a wet day happily engrossed in the task. My greatest difficulty is always in giving that last couple of turns to a screw, so that it goes sweetly home. A man has just that bit more strength to do the job, but this time I was shown how to use a pump screwdriver. Absolute magic! (But a tool to be treated with great respect.)

I stained the finished bookcase and was once again too impatient to get the books in situ – I didn't wait long enough for the stain to dry completely. Consequently, some of the books have faint brown edges on the bottom of their pages, where they drew up the stain. It gives them an antique finish which was not intended.

When I pass houses where a clear-out is obviously going on, and see trailers with wooden furniture and cupboards about to be dumped, I feel quite distraught. Useful timber, when dismantled, which should be in my shed! But if I put much more in it the door won't shut. You can't walk in, as it is, you have to climb over things, and it is then not nice to put your leg in a bucket of sugar beet, soaking for the ponies. I really need a small builders' yard, and a workshop. A friend said that I needed another house as well, in which to store furniture which I can't resist when offered. Very true, but I am learning, with anguish, to say no.

Here follows an idea which I am finding both useful and decorative.

Versailles tubs always look good in the garden, but commercial ones are hideously expensive. I was having a tidy-up in the garden shed last Easter, and I collected together a number of short lengths of tongue and groove-about eighteen inches long on average. I started to fiddle about with them, and saw that I had enough to make a box-shape, with the help of four corner mini-posts, and some bars to screw them onto at top and bottom. A plant tub began to take shape, but it lacked a bottom. Then I saw that if it was made without a bottom, I could drop all sorts of flowerpots or buckets of plants and bulbs inside it in their due season-a bottom wasn't necessary.

I put it together and gave it a coat of white emulsion paint. A rummage in my glory-box produced four wooden "acorns", sold as bannister finials at the DIY stores. One of these screwed to each corner and painted to match gave the finishing touch. My Versailles tub has been home all summer to hebe Autumn Glory, which is planted in a plastic bucket; now that it has finished flowering it is about to give way to a chrysanthemum, and it is a matter of seconds to switch things over.

Should you wish to copy this idea, make sure that the tongue and groove stands fractionally clear of the ground, while the corner posts stand on it without wobbles. This will help to keep the wood dry and preserve it when you water the plant. A pair of matching tubs would look even nicer-but I have now run out of tongue and groove.

Hedgehog's house is another well-used bit of DIY. I made it to encourage him to hibernate for another winter in my garden, but he chose not to, so all last winter it was empty. It was rather large, so in the early spring I took it to bits and remade it smaller. It is just a wooden box, with roofing felt over the top to keep out the wet, and it stands on half-bricks which are set into the ground so as to raise it just clear of the damp. Inside, I made a little enclosure in which to stand the pot of food.

I found that a roving animal – most probably a cat – was reaching in and hooking out the food, until I made this enclosure, but to make doubly sure of Hedgehog's privacy I devised a lean-to tunnel against the side of the house. I can remove this when I put in the food, but a cat can't get through it, or knock it aside, as I wedge it with a breeze block on top.

It amuses me that there is this unfailing ritual with a small animal. In goes his supper dish every night, piled high, and out comes the pot next day, licked clean as a whistle. Sometimes I stay quietly nearby, in the dusk, until I see him arrive, and then I can hear the busy tongue at work within. Once two arrived, and one morning I found the house crammed with greenery, and hoped it was going to be a nursery, but nothing came of that.

Should you wish to make a house for the use of your own private hedgehog, I think some sort of tunnel at the entrance is essential. Cats, and even urban foxes, will smell the food and they are agile creatures who will cleverly find a way to help themselves unless you take precautions. With hindsight, I also think that a lift-up top is a better idea, as it is easier to see to the food supply with this kind of access. I have to contort myself into a human question mark to do it, which is not ideal as it often involves kneeling on wet ground while a shrub drips steadily down my neck. I shall have to deal with this – when I have time.

Another useful bit of wet-day DIY was the conversion of a small table into a tea-trolley. All I had to do was to screw a rim all-round the top, using lengths of smooth-planed wood from the DIY store. These come in all lengths, shapes and sizes, so you are almost certain to find what you are looking for. Four small castors screwed to the legs made it mobile, and brass handles on each end gave the finishing touch. It would be good to be able to use it for tea by the fire, as was intended. It stands by a radiator, and the cats have commandeered it for warm snoozes.

I write of all this DIY so that you may know how easily and usefully and satisfyingly anyone of a practical nature can fill their time.

I have kept my "masterpiece" until last, although actually it was done eight years ago, in one of my wettest summer holidays.

Outside the back door was a porch, which had been temporarily renovated to improve what was a bit of an eyesore. I had often looked at it, together with the adjoining corner of the garden, and it seemed to me that here was the ideal spot for a small conservatory to extend a rebuilt porch.

I sent for brochures, and I went to look at conservatories in garden centres and show places. I soon found myself bewildered by the choices available. Charming young salesmen extolled their wares and the virtues of their ranges, from cedar-clad to all-over glazing. I saw pitched roofs and pointed roofs, end doors, sliding doors, and centre doors. I saw budget jobs ("Only £800, madam,") to super Victorian conservatories, the cost of which was tossed at me, nonchalantly, in thousands.

Each and every one had two snags. You've guessed the first – they were all too dear. The second was that they were all too big. My garden would be swamped. But once the idea took root, it wouldn't go away. Somewhere sheltered to sit, when it was too cold for the garden, was now a must.

I drove with a friend on one last trip to see an advertised "extensive range of garden buildings." One quick look round showed me that I had seen them all before, and that the range was by no means extensive, although this place had certainly extended a few of the prices. If you are going to buy a commercial job I do urge you to shop around-the difference in price-tags can mean quite a few extra pounds in your pocket.

Why is it, I wonder, that when I want something plain I can only find something fancy? In clothes, if I want blue, I can have any color but this. Nothing infuriates me more than to ask for a straightforward item and to be told (usually by a supercilious assistant barely out of rompers) that “there is no call for it now". Well, here was I calling loud and clear for a small conservatory, of a plain design, at a price that was reasonable, not something large and ornate that came "at about £3000, madam.”

"To hell with this,” I told my friend. “I'm going to build my own."

This was followed by a stunned silence. (Mine.) What had I said? And having said it, I knew that I must do it.

The next few days were spent in measuring my sheltered corner and consulting with a local builder, who agreed to rebuild the porch before my summer holiday began. It was to have a door at one end to give access for fuel deliveries, and a good-size window in the wall.

"And I want another door here,” I said, “and the side wall extended for eight feet.”

"Why?” asked Reg curiously.

"Because it is going to be the back wall of the conservatory which I am going to build,” I replied boldly.

If you say a thing often enough and firmly enough, you will eventually convince yourself. It is a curious fact that if you go round telling everyone you've got a cold or a pain, you will make it feel a lot worse. Keep quiet about it, and it won't seem half as bad. So now I began to believe that I was capable of undertaking this work and of achieving my end.

I went the rounds of builders’ merchants and, as always, received helpful advice and much interest. I needed to know what sizes and lengths of timber were available, and the dimensions of stone slabs for the floor, and where to get suitable glass. Then I went home and drew my design, and worked out the measurements.

When you begin to create something, you usually have to start by making a mess, and the preparation often takes longer than the actual job – as any home decorator will know. My conservatory was no exception to the rule. It was at once obvious that the pipe and drain from the kitchen sink would have to be lowered, in order that the stone slabs would cover it, so that the conservatory could sit on the slabs.

I took off the old pipe, and found out why the kitchen wall was damp at one end. The pipe was rusted and as full of holes as a colander. New plastic pipes and joining bits were bought. A shallow trench was dug and filled with rubble for the pipe to rest on. The top of the drain was hacked down to lower it a couple of inches, re-cemented (lovely cement!), and a flat lid found for the top. I marked the spot, so that one of the stone slabs could be cut for drain-inspection purposes.

Much encouraged by my progress on this initial job, I waited impatiently for my long holiday, so that I could begin in earnest.

How unkind the weather was, that holiday! It rained for half of every day except one, and on that one I had to go to a dentist for an emergency extraction. I had to get up extra early on dry mornings, to dig out the base for the stone slabs. It was hard work, because the ground was very stony. I went down about nine inches, and then got all the old stones and bricks that I could find and bashed them up for hard core. When it was well rammed down, I put a good layer of sand on top, and onto this went the slabs, on small dabs of cement. I have been known to argue with a spirit level, but on this occasion I worked carefully to its dictates. By the time I had finished heaving, levelling, and cutting the slabs where necessary, my back felt like a red-hot letter 'S'; I remember one occasion when sat on the sitting room floor, leaning against the wall, as I eased my tired muscles, over a stiff whisky. It was almost a case of "stand I up or lay I down, but don't bend I."

When the slabs had set, after a few days, it was lovely to walk out of the back door on to the firm, level base. Then I had my timber delivered, and treated every bit with preservative. There were six upright posts, four lengths for the base, eight lengths for joining the posts, and seven lengths for the rafters. There were also two uprights and four joining pieces for a door.

When I had the framework in position, I bought the glass for the roof, sides, and door. One attempt at cutting a pane resulted in shattered pieces, so I took the ones I wanted cut to a glazier and they were zipped to shape in a moment. I could watch an expert workman for hours.

I miscalculated the measurement of one pane, which had to fit an awkward angle, so I got a friend to take it back to the store, with the request that the man would cut it to a length of eighteen and a half inches. Back came the friend, and the glass, with the message that while the chap was most willing and able to cut glass smaller, he couldn't make it grow bigger. My pane was only eighteen and a quarter inches long. I re-checked – with a steel tape measure this time, not a linen one – and got the measurement right. No doubt when the chap recut the pane there was much mirth at my expense!

I admit to having a blind spot where figures are concerned. I can say one number to myself and write down something totally different, which makes DIY awkward at times. But eventually my conservatory stood almost complete, with its glass in the roof and sides, and the exterior finished at the bottom with tongue and groove. I spent a whole day making a cat-flap in this, for it is often the seemingly small details which take the longest. Many were the problems which I had to sort out along the way – but there it stood!

I thought the door would be easy, and so it was, to make. The trouble was that after it was hung, it kept on dropping so that it dragged on the floor, and nothing I did would stop this.

"Think of a square made of bits of meccano," said the pub landlord. "If you hold it by one side, it will sag until you brace it with a cross-piece." So a clever friend of his measured and cut a piece of timber for me, which was shaped to fit across the bottom of the door, from corner to corner, and it has never dragged since.

Then my hard-working "holiday" was over, and I went away to work. I left everything waterproof. I came back the next weekend to find rain dripping everywhere through the roof.... the blue tits had peeked out most of the putty. (I never did cure this problem, and in the end I had to put sheets of rigid plastic over the glass.)

The ideal way to tackle a big job, such as this was for an amateur, would be to build a trial one first. That way, one would discover the snags and solve many problems before embarking on the real thing. One of my big mistakes was in not pitching the roof more steeply, to help water run-off. And I have still not achieved a satisfactory door catch. A bales catch jammed in wet weather, when the wood swelled. I also found that a line of damp kept creeping in round the bottom when it rained, but this is now hidden by a vinyl floor covering, which I put down because the bare stone slabs looked a bit stark, It is not affected by minor damp.

A marble topped table and two chairs stand under the window, where one can eat pleasant al fresco meals. A half-round table full of plants stands on one side of the door, and a low table covered with a marble slab, also laden with plants, stands against the back wall. Two small armchairs just fit in, and a lantern and a small round moonlight make this a lovely place to linger, on warm summer nights. It is frostproof, except for really hard ones, so the plants stay green all the year round.

So here I sit, eight years on, with the sun streaming through the open door, and the warmth trapped, while the chilly breeze is excluded. Of all the things which I have done, or may yet do, this is one of the and most used. I often smile when I think of those "only £800, madam," jobs. My conservatory cost me about £200.

An amusing postscript to all this came when I sent a photograph and a brief account of how I did it to a garden magazine. This earned me a tenner, followed by a letter forwarded from an admiring lady in Cornwall. She would like to build her own conservatory too, and how did she start?

I sent her some notes, a sketch, and advice, wished her good luck, and told her to write and let me know how she got on. I heard no more, so my "fan" probably never got started.

*The original conservatory as built by Liz*

# Break Of Day

I often wake, briefly, at dawn but something made me wake up extra early one morning.

Outside it was still almost dark, with that 'thin' darkness of summer as opposed to the jet black of a winter night. I could see the shape of the hill outlined against the sky, and make out the dark mass of trees. Getting out of bed, I opened the window wide. Not a sound, except the occasional faint rustle of the breeze in the bushes opposite. The air had a cool freshness that was inviting... and suddenly I was wide awake.

"You're mad," I told myself as I dressed.

Quietly I let myself out, so as not to disturb my neighbours. The car started at the first go, and I drove off slowly, hoping that no-one in the hotel would hear and think that I was a guest slipping off without paying the bill. (Oh, yes, that happens – they call them Runners). No-one was up in the village, and nobody's lights were on. I had it all to myself, a sleeping world whose day had not yet dawned.

Turning right, I drove up to the moor, and there I parked. The air was quite cold up here, and I was glad of my coat. Imperceptibly, the night had already paled and I could see my way easily along the track. Overhead, the sky was misty and the stars were tangled in it, the merest pinpoints of light here and there.

I looked about eagerly... for deer, for badgers, for foxes, for an owl slipping along the hedgerow, or a hare loping away. Nothing. Nobody not even a sheep or a pony. This truly was solitude.

There is such a thing as the sound of silence. I experienced it there. It is, first of all, the absence of sounds which you notice.

There were no bird cries, no hoots from a distant owl or calls between companionable rocks, who are early risers. There were no farmyard noises – a gate banging, or the clang of metal striking metal. Civilised life had ceased to intrude. No dog barked, no-one whistled. There were no faint rumbles from a distant 'plane. Between the rustles made by puffs of breeze in the hedge, there was this other thing – an intangible presence that felt as still water must feel to a fish, enveloping, calm, elemental... the sound of silence.

I walked along in this mystical hour when time was poised between, the night and day. Presently a strong smell of honey reached my nose, and I quested up and down the stretch of rough cart track from whence it came. There was a broken-edged hole in the side of it, and stooping down I found quite a few dead bees around it. Here was a puzzle; had a fox or badger been attracted by the smell, and dug out a small colony of honeybees? Swarms escape from beekeepers from time to time. One had settled and thrived for years in a nearby church roof; another still lives high up in a hollow oak on the roadside a mile or two from the cottage. Perhaps this one was an escapee too; if so, it had now come to an end, as there were no live bees left, and not a trace of honeycomb, only that lingering, delicious smell. I hope some small creature got the benefit, and gave himself a treat. But I wonder who?

Now the hills around me were all outlined against a silvery sky, and in the east was a flush of pink. I walked on, the sole occupant of this cool and lovely world. The night creatures had obviously all gone home to bed, and the morning ones were not up yet. The moor rolled away on either hand, and I went as far as the stream which crosses the track at the bottom of the slope, before turning back.

I was facing north-east now, so I had the bright splendour of the dawn before me, growing steadily into a liquid radiance that some of the great Italian painters have caught so well. Caught, but not completely, for nothing can ever entirely hold that living glow of golden, rose-flushed light that changes with every passing moments. Even as I turned away to look down into a small combe (still hoping for creature company), the light had grown brighter, and the darkness had dwindled into mist, gathered in the hollows. The vaporous sky was forming into shreds of pinkish cloud, and it was now day.

Surely there will at least be rabbits about, I asked myself? But I walked all the way back to the car without seeing one. Clearly, I had been too late for one lot and too early for the other lazy blighters.

A couple of village early risers looked startled as I drove past. I wondered what they would think. Perhaps that I had been for a night on the tiles? They would probably be relieved to see who it was, because more than once an early car has meant trouble. There have been burglaries and break-ins at the post office, the shop, the pub, the village hall, and several guest houses in recent consecutive years. So I waved, boldly advertising myself, whatever might be the wild surmises.

Back home, it was now a lovely summer morning, and still only six o'clock. I had a sharp appetite and breakfast was very welcome. Then I rolled up my sleeves and set about painting all the ready-washed woodwork in the sitting room. It was all done by ten o'clock.

I made a cup of coffee, and then took a very indignant dog out for a walk. I had committed the unforgiveable sin of going out, on my own, and the outburst of barks, off-lead in the field, clearly expressed a ticking-off.

It was worth it, though. To be so alone, in such a silent world, was an experience to be remembered with gratitude. It cost so little

– only the effort – and the gift of the daybreak had been mine. No matter that I hadn't glimpsed any of the shy inhabitants of the moor, although some of them might have been watching me from their hide-outs. I had seen the dawn of a new day out of eternity, which had never been before, and would never come again.

What more awesome experience can there be than that?

# Visitors

I stayed in an old schoolhouse on my first visit to North Devon, many years ago. The piping and twittering of the children as they arrived for school woke me up, and I looked out of the bedroom window to see them straggling down the steep drive, and climbing the field path to the playground entrance. The little girls wore sunbonnets. (This is not a give-away as to how long ago it was, but shows how the old-fashioned ways lingered on here.)

The school was built in 1905 for forty-five children, and owed much to the support of the family in the local "big house." It is an attractive building, with the headteacher's house attached to the school room. In its closing years it was in the devoted hands of a Yorkshire woman and her daughter, and a local woman paid them an unsolicited tribute.

"I'm sure it's thanks to them," she said to me, "that there are so many nice people in the valley, who went to that school as children."

The last schoolmarm, (the daughter), received the MBE for her services. It was she with whom I stayed, on that first visit. The school closed down in 1971, due to the fall in the child population, when there were only about seven left of an age to attend.

During the very bad winter of 1962-3, when the village and its surroundings were snowbound for six weeks, school was held in the pub, for those who could be got there by conscientious parents. The old locals don't really value education, even now.

"'Tis only book learning," they say.

The children are now collected by bus and taken to school five miles away, like visitors from outer space. This is happening all over the country, but it's rather sad, when the valley once supported no less than three small schools, if "The Old Schoolhouse", and "The Schoolroom", properties at either end of the valley, are named in accordance with their history.

Now that the children mix more widely and television has brought the world into their homes, I wonder if the pull away from rural life will accelerate. Perhaps the children themselves will grow up to value an education, as a means to a different kind of life. There are few opportunities for them in farming hereabouts, as many of the farms employ only one permanent worker. Other work is contracted out, or relies on casual labour.

When the area was even more isolated, before it had good roads and transport, some notable visitors found their way here. Daniel Defoe was one; the poet, Shelley was another in 1812. He, Wordsworth and Coleridge, nearly decided to settle locally, where "Shelley's Cottage" is now a guest house. Southey, walking on Exmoor, took refuge from storm in one of Porlock's inns, and it was in Porlock that Blackmore wrote part of "Lorna Doone". I find it strange that Gainsborough, who also visited the area, was not to my knowledge moved to put some of its dramatic scenery on canvas. Come to think of it, I don't think any of the "greats" have done so.

Some "fishy" visitors to these shores were the herrings, from the Middle Ages until the fish left these coasts in the 17th century. We get another type of fishy visitor in the summer season nowadays – those who steal out of their hotel in the very small hours, and leave the landlord with an unpaid bill. These "runners" have increased in recent years, and the police say that the motorways have helped this type of criminal along with all the others that use quick get-away tactics. But how mean – to talk and eat and socialise with bona fide guests as their equal, and then to sneak off!

"The visitors" are now one of North Devon's economic mainstays. How this industry has grown! I have stayed in many of the hotels and guest houses and farms over the years, and found them all spotless and comfortable. Sometimes I see a strapping young man driving a tractor through the village; one day I told him that I still recall him as an angelic-looking toddler with blue eyes and golden curls, a muddy face and minute wellies, laughing as his father told him, "You'm wicked." I stayed in that farmhouse several times.

There was a charm about such places then that today's visitors no longer enjoy. Most were lit by oil lamps, whose soft warm glow and gentle hiss were companionable in the evenings. They made pools of light that were far more beautiful than the glare of electricity.

The visitors always got the best parlour, but I liked to get myself into the kitchen, where usually there was a high-backed settle, black with age, and a kettle singing on the side of a huge range. The windows were small, the curtains faded, and the centerpiece of the room was always a big, solid table, made to seat a one-time farmer's family that spanned several generations. Through the door, in a pantry, one might catch a glimpse of bowls of cream standing on cool, slate shelves.

The visitors' bedroom had a wash-hand stand with ewers and bowls that have become collectors' pieces today, often with a matching "potty" under the bed. The snowy bedclothes, stiff and smelling of cleanliness, felt snowy too, but when one cautiously wriggled exploratory toes they would meet the comfort of a stone hot water bottle. Amazingly, they too are collectors' items now.

Today's visitors no doubt appreciate all mod. cons, with electric fires, and running h and c in the bedrooms. The kitchens are probably fitted ones, whose like may be encountered anywhere... and the old, simple charm has gone forever. No amount of hanging up strings of onions, fake warming pans, and bunches of dried flowers can evoke the lost atmosphere of homely living.

Visitors are often the source of amusement. One Sunday morning recently, we regulars in the congregation were taken aback by the antics of a large group of them. They were of an evangelical persuasion, and at one point in the service, where the booklet says, "All may exchange a sign of peace," they leapt up. We avoided each other's eyes as they scuttled about grabbing and shaking hands with all and sundry. Thank goodness they didn't go in for kissing, too.

(I am reminded of a true story of a visitor who was taken to church by friends of mine. He was unused to churchgoing, and when at the communion rail, he took literally the words, "Drink ye all of this and passed the Cup back, empty.)

Curiosity prompted me to go and look in the visitors' book of another church, a famous little one not far away. I was astounded. In the first eight months of the year, people had come to look around it from all over the British Isles, from every country in Europe, and from Canada, New Zealand, America, South Africa, Russia, Australia, Tanzania, Hong Kong, Japan, Malaysia, Saudi Arabia, Malta, Afghanistan, Barbados, and Nigeria. And not every visitor signs the book, so there may well have been other countries represented. I was glad to see that some other summer visitors are still coming — the swallows which nest in the church porch.

I have lost count of the visitors who call on me. A hospitable nature is always at variance with a love of solitude. I was once asked when was a good time to call, and replied, "There isn't one." What I meant was that whatever the time, I will always be doing something. However, I am very good at stitching a garden-party smile on my face, and saying How Nice To See You, even if I am grinding my molars at being dragged away from whatever it was.

How about this for a coincidence? An old colleague wrote and asked for the date of a member of staff's wedding, so I went to the phone box and gave it to him. Just as he was saying, "We'd love to come down and see you," the pips went and I hastily yelled, "No more money," and thought I'd got away with it. Next day, I was sitting in the garden writing to a friend, and describing gleefully how I had dodged issuing an invitation. As I wrote those very words, there was a rattle at the side door – and there they were!

This friend to whom I was writing was invited to spend a few days at the cottage some years ago. He is good company, but full of restless energy, and so the visit was somewhat tiring. During it, I had just taken up early morning tea when we heard a loud crash. We stared at each other, aghast, and then I said, "I'll bet that's the ceiling over the stair!" (I hadn't yet put the false one over the old plaster).

*Liz and Peter Ball in the conservatory*

I went to look, but the ceiling was still in situ, so we both went downstairs. A nasty mess greeted us in the kitchen. A wall cupboard had broken away from its brackets and crashed to the floor, and there were all the pots and jars and bags of things strewn far and wide, with jam oozing everywhere.

My bachelor friend took one look, and said, "Gosh! I'm off!" and went back to bed!

I don't hold it against him, really. Bachelors are inclined to be selfish. But he hasn't been asked to stay since!

One sunny afternoon I decided that a bit of nude sunbathing was in order. I got out my sunbed and arranged a large sunshade at the head as an added screen. My garden is totally secluded at the house end, unless anyone strains to look over the fence, and one can always hear people approaching as their footsteps crunch in the gravel drive.

Woozling blissfully, this is just what I heard between waking and sleeping. Alas, the masculine-sounding footsteps were coming my way, so I made myself long and thin and clutched the sunshade firmly overhead. The following conversation took place.

"Excuse me, madam."

"Yes?"

"Can you tell me where the next door garden begins?"

"Just over the wall."

"Which wall would that be?"

"I'll point. Can you see my arm?"

"YES, madam."

"I hope that's all you can see?"

"Oh, yes, madam."

I indicated, and the footsteps went away again. But, as someone pointed out, how was he so sure it was madam in the first place?

Now that most people have a car, or use the weekly bus for shopping trips, there are few regular delivery services to the village. We used to have a fish man, who was very enterprising, with an immaculate van and fish packed in crushed ice. He announced his arrival with an old brass school bell, and my cats soon learnt to gather round expectantly. He deserved to get on because he used his initiative, and if I was out he would leave me something for them tucked securely behind the door. His day began very early indeed, but something called the "quota system" beat him in the long run. He couldn't get the supplies he wanted, and it was a sad day when he announced his last trip.

"It's just not worth the hassle," he said. "I'm going back to the building trade."

So now we have to go nearly twenty miles for a good choice of wet fish, even though we live within sight of the sea. It is indeed a mad modern world.

For those who wanted her there was also a travelling hairdresser who came every week, but Caro is now juggling a baby instead of a hair dryer, and comes no more. That only leaves one regular weekly van visiting the village – at the time of writing – other than pub deliveries, and that is the mobile library. This excellent service is a lifeline to some, and the number of books on display is surprisingly large. I shall be happy to use it if and when I can no longer drive a car to the library and am reduced to a tricycle.

On Sunday afternoons a knock on the door used sometimes to mean the unwelcome attentions of Jehovah's witnesses. Nothing infuriates me more than having my peace disturbed by these persistent arguers. I try to be polite as I close the door firmly upon them, but one of my visitors had a better idea. He answered the door for me, as I guessed who was there, and said cheerfully, "Thank you for calling, but we're Muslims here." They haven't been back since.

One evening some friends who called were most amused at a rather muffled knock, followed by a thump, on the front door.

"That's Ben," I said, and went into the kitchen for his biscuit.

He was a collie and lived at the farm down the road. I don't know how he learnt to call like it, but he did, regularly, and later on Sal followed suit. I loved her, and used to give her a plate of titbits, as she was very thin. Ben died, and Sal no longer leaves Tam's side, but occasionally Mitch comes up from the same farm and hovers if he sees me. He always takes his biscuit all the way home before eating it. I love all my canine callers dearly, and they are never unwelcome.

When you stand on the headland you get a marvellous view of any shipping in the Channel. One sees tankers, dredgers, and container ships on their way to the Welsh ports or Avonmouth, and in summer there are yachts and an assortment of holiday fishing boats. A paddle steamer still makes a few trips, but when I was a child the sparkling white Campbell's steamer was a regular visitor along the Channel. You could embark in the heart of Bristol and go down the Avon, across to Barry, and back to Clevedon, Lynmouth or Ilfracombe. It was on one of these that Farmer Jack and I made our trip around Lundy Island. They have been a part of the summer sea traffic for so long that it will be the end of an era if they ever cease to run.

An old car rally paid a regular summer visit to the valley, though I haven't seen this for a couple of years. The quaint little box-shaped vehicles chugged steadily along, each one obviously tended with loving care, judging by the gleaming brass and upholstery, and each one worth a bomb, so I'm told. Occasionally someone drives a very smart pony and trap through the village, and all heads turn. It is sometimes hired for a wedding, and this year the poor little bride was unlucky enough to have a downpour on her way to church. When we romanticize about the old forms of transport we are apt to overlook the discomforts.

When the coach ran from Minehead to Lynmouth, the men passengers were asked to get out and walk on the steepest hills, and if the going was really difficult – such as in icy weather, I suppose – all the ladies under forty might be asked to do likewise. This invariably emptied the coach of nearly all the lady passengers.

We get a steady trickle of campers in the summer who use two or three fields here and there, but since the pub changed hands we have had scouts in the field behind the cottage. Their camp site is immaculate, both during and after their stay, and delicious smells float across from their cooking every evening. Last year one solitary little girl was with them, her tent discreetly distanced from the rest.

She came across to the fence to have a chat with me one day, and said that she was enjoying herself. If the boys got a bit rough she went to bed early and read a book.

"And sometimes," she said, "they tell rude stories when they're in bed. I try to listen, and some of them are quite funny, really."

Scouts, like everything else, have changed since my young days. They don't appear to have any ceremony at the ending of the day, or church parade, or a singsong round the campfire. And their language amongst themselves, which I occasionally overhear, is a disgrace. Individually, however, they have always spoken politely to me, and I wish that this cult of crudeness could die an instant death.

There are a few well-known people from T.V. and the pop scene who have homes in the area. They must once have come to visit and fallen in love with what they saw, and later on bought properties with the added bonus of privacy. Their houses are tucked away in lonely corners, and as far as I know, the privacy is respected, so I shan't disclose any names. When limelight is your bread and butter, seclusion must be your caviar!

Some American visitors to the area were petrified at the gradients on one of our famous hill roads. The occasion was a very elaborate wedding, when guests came from all over the place and were boarded out in various hotels locally. A team of helpers was enlisted to act as drivers for a fleet of hired mini-buses, and for a few days our quiet lanes hummed with activity.

Marquees and tents were hired from London, as were the florists who "did" the decor, and we were all agog as snippets of news filtered back, via the helpers.

"'You wouldn't know it was a marquee – it's got four chandeliers in it,"

"Half the band's got drunk already."

"The wedding was nearly off last night – the bridegroom had a blazing row with his prospective father-in-law in a pub car park."

I knew several of the minibus drivers, and was given a graphic description of one load of Yanks who were fetched from Taunton station. They were rather brash and noisy, and had a mountain of luggage, so they were packed in like sardines.

"Say, I'll ride shotgun with you, driver," bawled one, scrambling into the front seat.

"Gee, is this trap safe?" queried another.

"You sure we'll get there? The springs aint too great!"

Reassuring his passengers, the driver set off along the winding route, fielding all the comments as to the quaintness of the cottages and farms they passed. Then they came to a notorious hill, where the road steepens steadily.

"Mac, I sure hope your brakes are good."

"Are we gonna have to come back the same way?"

Then they came to the bend, where the road takes a flying leap upwards.

"Holy COW!" came the yell.

Quite a few people from the valley have been to Buckingham Palace.

Mary and Bert were known to me, and they were invited to one of the Garden Parties because of his work for the British Legion. Naturally, what we all wanted to know was Did You See The Queen, but Mary, bless her heart, was more keen on describing in detail the outfit which she wore.

"And the hat," she said, "Was a model and cost six pounds," which in those days was going it!

The other lady known to me, who was honoured, was the schoolmarm, who received the MBE. She recounted her visit with deep appreciation, from the moment when a wheelchair was swiftly and tactfully offered for her ailing husband (whom she had married late in life) to the put-you-at-your-ease briefing which all the recipients were given, and finally to the moment of presentation to Her Majesty.

"The band played the March of the Siamese Children, from "The King and I," "and the queen was lovely," she said. "She asked me, 'Now let me see, your work was with children, wasn't it?' She made everyone feel relaxed – it was just like a family party."

*Liz was a great letter writer and kept in touch with family members wherever they were, in this photo cousins Sam and Huck visiting from their home in New York to catch up in person.*

So though we may be a bit isolated here, the big world has heard us.

Of all the visitors who have stayed at the pub-cum-hotel, some stick in my mind who no longer come. One was a millionaire who made his money from scrap metal. He left a sum with the landlord so that old Jor, who was blind, should always have his daily pint, and many a time I have seen this carried down the road to his lodgings by the bar man.

*Huck especially enjoyed exploring the garden*

Another was something important to do with a national newspaper, whose wife wore rings of surpassing beauty. They flashed with the fire of costly purity whenever she moved her hands.

Last year I missed Andrew and his wife, and feared the worst. They both have cancer, and I was happy to see them again this year. Andrews's condition has stabilised, and his wife fights on with cheerful courage. She looks so white, but always has a smile of greeting. Isn't that often the way of things? Those who have the worst to contend with show the greatest grit. We are trying to get Andrew started with white Japanese anemones; he can grow the pink ones, but the white just fade away. Those I grew in a pot for him two years ago have followed all the others, yet here they flourish like weeds. I always think of this couple when they are in flower and mentally wish them well.

One visitor whose presence seems to be getting very spasmodic is the cuckoo. How curious it is that we think of this bird's call as the epitome of an English spring and summer, when it is a "foreigner". I have only heard it two or three times this year, soft and far away, like "the horns of elfland faintly blowing".

The swallows, too, have been fewer in number, and the bad weather has been blamed for causing many casualties in the migration to these shores. Is the cuckoo a similar victim? Or has it, I wonder, something to do with the destruction of hedgerow nesting sites, so that this so-welcome visitor can no longer find sufficient hosts for her eggs?

A newcomer to the nuts hanging near the kitchen window in recent weeks has been a greater spotted woodpecker. This beautiful bird, a young female, has pecked her fill only a few feet away, so that I have been able to study her markings. Her rump and wedge-shaped tail are pressed against the nuts to balance her as she rams in that long beak. When she has finished – and she doesn't hesitate to use that beak to repel all boarders – she flies up to the nearby telegraph pole for a pause, before going about her other business. Her visits have been regular, morning and evening, and I've looked forward to them. Her black and white back, creamy front, chestnut rump, and scarlet poll, which only young birds have, are very striking.

I think the winter will come early this year. We have had a poor summer, following an equally poor spring when there wasn't sufficient sun and warmth to make the crocus open wide their cups or draw out the scent of the snowdrops. Now, as summer moves towards its end, then have been some lovely sunny days, but the nights are chilly. The dew each morning is a cold mantle laid over everything.

Perhaps because of this, fewer butterflies have visited the garden this summer. There are at least thirteen thousand known species throughout the world; of our British ones, I have missed the tortoiseshells, the red admirals, the painted ladies, and peacocks. What exquisite creatures they are, drifting, hovering, settling with wings a-quiver as each long probosis uncurls and sips deeply of the nectar in the chosen flower. Some of these fragile-looking butterflies actually migrate, and cross the English Channel. I find that amazing when I study those delicate wings. If one alights on your hand, it is weightless, and yet it is capable of as such a sustained effort as that.

Have you ever sat in your garden and watched a hummingbird hawk moth at work? It is a day-flying moth, and its wings beat so fast that they are a blur as it hovers in front of the flower. It inserts its proboscis as the hummingbird does its beak, without alighting. A pause a flick, a dart... and so it moves on.

What miracles of creation these things are! I look at Hedgehog, with all his prickles, and I think of creatures like elephants and giraffes, and tiny things that live in the sea, and the countless birds and scurrying insects. Never, in a billion years, could we have designed a world so crammed with such diverse forms of life!

# Midsummer Madness

There came a night when it would have been a crime to stay in and go to bed. The moon was bathing everything in soft light, transforming the world into a waking dream of silver, grey and pewter. Just so do we perceive it in our sleep... only now it was calling me to activity. In short, to go out for a walk.

I called for my neighbour at the shop, whose downstairs lights showed that she had not yet gone to bed.

"Come up on the moor," I invited. "This is too good to waste."

She looked distraught. "I can't. I'd love to, but I can't. I'm doing the VAT accounts."

What hells we have created for ourselves in this modern world! Here was this beautiful night, crying out for exploration, and she had to stay in and do accounts to meet a deadline. Soon we shall no longer dare to be ourselves, we shall be regulated to within an inch of our lives!

I turned away sadly, and then decided to take the dog and go on my own. Such silvery radiance was not to be missed. Rick – for it was his day – was overjoyed. He loved going out at night. He barked, as usual, all the way up to the moor, thus advertising that I was doing something odd again.

It was as bright as day up there. I looked at that luminous disc, floating like a pearl in the sky, and marvelled that men had actually stood and walked on its surface. I remembered how the astronauts had said how beautiful the earth looked, from space. And here was I, a minute speck of life, moving across an infinitesimal portion of it, thinking, feeling, and wondering at it –"dwellers all in time and space".

There were sheep faintly bleating ahead, and a group of ponies detached themselves from a cluster of gorse bushes and trotted away. Rick disappeared into an ashen bed of bracken, his shadow vanishing behind him. I could see the occasional gleams of car headlights on the distant coast road, and in a gap between shoulders of the moor the sea showed darkly. On its far side the lights of the Welsh coast sparkled in a jewelled strand. It was truly a beautiful night. How glad I was that I hadn't got to stay in and do my VAT!

And then my imagination began to stir.

Now, a good imagination is a wonderful thing, but not when you suddenly find yourself dwelling on, and enlarging upon, the unexplainable. What triggered it off was passing near a cottage which lay in a hollow to my left. I looked down on it and remembered the night of its fire.

Two friends, one of whom owned the cottage, had come to it for a short stay, and one of them, an old acquaintance had walked down to see me in the evening. They had forgotten to bring milk, and asked if I had a spare pint. After he'd gone, I saw that he'd left it behind on the kitchen table, so I thought that I would take it up to them early next morning.

When I got there, I immediately saw a blackened porch. "They've had a fire in it," I thought. And then my eyes lifted to the roof, and with horror I saw the charred and jagged rafters rearing up, the broken windows, and twisted frames gaping wide. I shall never forget picking my way through the tangled mess inside the shell of the building. I called their names – but I fully expected to find two charred bodies.

Mercifully, they had got out in time and gone home, the fire brigade had put out the blaze in the night, but how it started remains a mystery to this day. Foul play was suspected, because

Ivan had loved another man's wife; nothing was ever proved, however.

As I looked down on it, rebuilt but empty, the cottage seemed very unlike the scene of violent passion and crime. But the thought of it stirred sudden shudder.

I thought of another mystery. An old inn not far away had recently had some interior alterations done. It dated back to the sixteenth century, and the workmen, in removing a wall, had uncovered a skeleton. What ancient ghastly deed was thus exposed? It was unsolvable, of course after all those years.

I had intended to drive the long way home, and make a circular trip, but to do so I would have to pass along a dark stretch of road near the church. Even one of the incumbents had said that there was "something" just here. "He walks towards the church," he said.

No thank you. Not that way.

Calling the dog, I went back to the car. I would, of course, remember at this lonely moment the several accounts of footsteps walking along an empty corridor at the pub! The landlord, most practical and down-to-earth of men, had looked up from the bar one night, just before he closed and bolted the doors, to see a monkish figure standing in the corner.

"But we had him exorcised," 'he said cheerfully, afterwards. "Father E. did it, and I've never seen it since."

Suddenly the moonlit world seemed less than friendly, and tinged with the unexplainable. Its chilly light was ghostly, a thin veil between the solid world and... what? Suppose, now, the dog began to howl, backing away from nothing with hackles raised, as they have many times been seen to do?

But Rick, bless him, bounded up at that moment with sparkling eyes and a cold nose, wet with dew and full of life and joy at his unexpected treat. When we got into the car he shook himself, and the drops flew all over me in a cold shower.

That cured an errant imagination.

I drove back to the welcoming warmth of the cottage, whose white walls gleamed in moonlight made beautiful again by the familiar things of home. Now I could feel pity for all poor ghosts, for unquiet spirits, and those who met with violent ends. Life, as George Barrow said, is so sweet. "There's night and day, brother, both sweet things; sun, moon, and stars, brother, all sweet things; there's likewise a wind on the heath. Life is very sweet, brother; who would wish to die?"

# The Social Round

"Whatever will you do all day, when you retire to a place like that?"

I've quoted that remark before, but really – it still makes me laugh. There is so much going on all the time that the socially minded could, as I once heard the milkman say, "be out every bloody night of the week". I think he was, because he drank away his house and money and went bust, and now we don't have a milkman in the village anymore.

Before I came to live here permanently, I remember going to a slide show in the village hall, put on for the visitors by a skilled photographer of the red deer. The slides were magnificent, the result of hours and hours of patient watching; he knew many of the deer as individuals, and gave them names. When he came to one slide of a beautiful stag with a proudly borne set of antlers, and said, "Old Father Time-taken yesterday," meaning killed by the hunt, a lone voice called out, "Shame!"

Heads turned, and there was a startled silence. It was I. Thus, involuntarily, did I nail my colours to the mast long ago. To see these creatures at peace, and then to think of the stress and disruption and fear that man causes them sickens me still. Why can't people see the pattern and design in the universe, where all things have their place, and where we, "the crown of creation", have a responsibility for every living thing? Even for the earth itself, whose fertility is becoming ever more fragile under our mismanagement.

My cry of, "Shame" immediately labelled me, and it stuck. Ivan was walking along the lane to call on me recently, when a car drew up and a farmer's wife asked him where he was going. He told her that he was coming to see me.

"Good God," she said. "You know she's anti-hunt?"

A naturalist society occasionally puts on a slide show of the flora and fauna of the area, and they also do conducted walks which are very popular. They hold an open afternoon in the summer at a naturalist centre, where I have personally sampled the most sumptuous of laid-on teas, as well as admired the exhibits.

A thriving village art group takes to the out-of-doors in summer, and presently puts on a display of all the work. A retired late vicar and his wife were two people who took up painting from scratch, and their skill developed by leaps and bounds, their paintings selling readily.

A couple of years ago, the village hall was burgled during the exhibition, and many of the items were stolen. The police found the floor littered with spent matches, and thanks to a neighbour's wakeful night, when he was drinking tea in the garden at three a.m., and heard a car, they were able to piece together a useful pattern of events. I think a few of the pictures were recovered, on sale, some-where eventually.

There is a horticultural society which holds meetings and talks not far away, and they too put on a show in the summer. There are gardens both great and small to visit round about, displaying that magical sign, "Garden Open Today." Who can pass one by?

For the horsey folk, the summer is crammed with events. There are point-to-points, ghymkhanas, and shows, and a lot of these activities spring from local hunts. I fail to see why they couldn't continue, if the hunts turned to drag-hunting, instead of the pursuit of live animals. Nowadays, there are only two complete months in the year here- June and July- when there isn't some form of hunting going on. But opposition to it is growing steadily, and the voice of the "antis" grows more persistent. I was delighted to hear of a pack of draghounds not far away, recently.

Pony trekking across the moors has increased in popularity, and there are holidays advertised which are based on this. Until recently we had a group regularly staying in the village overnight, and it was a joy to see the condition of the animals and the discipline with which the operation was conducted. Every rider dismounted and led his animal through the village, and the grooms who had preceeded them were waiting to check over and feed them, before putting on their coats and turning them into the fields overnight.

Ben quite enjoyed the company, and appeared to show them round, leading the string of visitors up and down, and helping himself liberally to the piles of fodder placed here and there by the grooms. This is called horsage, and has a pleasant, rich, spicey smell. The owner of this string would gaze at Ben with disfavour.

"He doesn't need it," he would say. "He's gross!"

I must admit that when the grass is lush, both Ben and Katie look rather rotund.

When I used to attend the tiny church up the valley, I enjoyed the occasional sherry parties after the service which the then-incumbent liked to give. What a man he was! He had lived a full and varied life and held some distinguished posts, and I never heard him give a sermon which didn't make me think.

He was the only man who announced a hymn, in the Guards' Chapel, which wasn't even in the book. And it was he who, one Mothering Sunday, thought that all the ladies should receive posies, not just the mothers, and stripped the altar of flowers for them. Can you imagine it?

"Have some flowers", he said, and thrust them with stalks still dripping, into the hands of the childless, while the "flower ladies" watched the wrecking of their arrangements with frozen dismay.

He was dearly-loved, and would radiate hospitality as he did the rounds of his sherry party guests. The rectory is a modern and for once beautiful building, within which his pieces of old family furniture and portraits were well displayed. He lost a lot of his silver in a burglary while he was conducting a morning service, but nothing could daunt his spirit, not even his failing health, or quench his love of people.

In the visitors season there is an indoor bowls tournament at the village hall, which I am told is good fun. A friend and I were once asked to go and be helpers, as someone on the rota couldn't manage to come, so we agreed. We presented ourselves early at the door, only to be greeted chillingly by "Lady" Hold.

"YES?" she enquired.

"We've come to take the tickets at the door," we said. "Someone can't come tonight."

"I am taking the tickets," said Lady H. "But you can go and help those boys down there to set up the skittles, if you like."

She waved us loftily away. My friend gave me A Look, and we turned as one and marched home again. And that is how Mrs. Hold got her nickname.

Flower festivals and fates are legion in the summer, all of them crying out for helpers and cake-makers. The local newssheet likewise puts out its pleas for team-mates to help with its compiling, folding and distribution. No-one need ever be lonely or want for company, or lack a purposeful activity. You like to sing? There's a choral society as well as church choirs. Flower arranging? There's a group. Bellringing? Weekly practices. The list is endless, especially for those who are evening class minded, and are prepared to travel a few miles. And for the very energetic, there are charity runs from time to time in summer. There is also the semilocal show-cum-gymkhana, and later on, The Sale, which I have previously mentioned.

A new annual event takes place after the cricket season ends. The buyer of the "big house" set out to be The Squire, and provided a cup for the competing teams, which I saw presented at the Cricket Dinner.

This dinner was an amusing event for me, because I knew the housekeeper and she asked me to join the team of women who were to be helpers, for a bit of fun. I got there early on the night and was given a quick tour to see the latest additions to the house.

Pots of orchids at £30 a time were everywhere. Orchids were fashionable, the in-thing in all the glossies, so they sat on all the windowsills. A huge portrait of the owner now decorated the wall over the staircase, its frame and surface cleverly curved to fit the bend. A tiny courtyard had been spruced up to house a white wrought iron table and four chairs, patterned with fern fronds. I didn't ask the price of those!

As I was helping to put salads in bowls at the vast kitchen table, in came the owner's wife and I was introduced, by prior arrangement, as "a lady from the village." I had been dared to pose as a real Devonian with an accent to match, so I did.

"And 'ow du 'ee like living down 'ere, then?" I asked "Tis summat different from London for 'ee, intit?"

"Er-oh, yes," Came the stilted reply.

"Oh, 'ess, and tis fair to say if you'm 'ere when the snow comes, 'twill be an eye-opener for 'ee. Proper job that'llbe, to get 'ee up that drive then, you!"

"Er, yes," she murmured again, and faded out quickly, while squeaks became shrieks of laughter behind me.

I enjoyed waiting on the local populace, who looked surprised to see me, and who played up well when I lavished Sirs and

Madams on them. Then there was the "Squire's" speech before the cup was presented. It wavered between the pompous and the vernacular, so that a few bloodies were scattered throughout to get a laugh. There was polite, if unenthusiastic applause, before everyone went back to the well-filled plates of delicious nosh. It only goes to show that "instant roots" is a commodity not to be found, let alone bought, however deep the pocket.

As the year moves on, with its ever-increasing number of coffee mornings, jumble sales, and car-boot sales, the social round takes more to the indoor. Whist drives begin, and in October there are Harvest Suppers everywhere. I think that weight-watching must be an occupational hazard with the clergy.

One event, for which coach trips are arranged, is Bridgwater Carnival. This is one of the biggest affairs in Europe, and on occasions. I have been caught up in its traffic, when travelling down at the weekend. The parade of floats gets bigger and more elaborate every year, and those who brave the crowds, and often the weather, rave about it. The work involved in planning and making the floats is more or less non-stop from one year to the next, and it is now a major event in the West country calendar.

In November there is Bonfire Night at the pub. There was sometimes a bonfire lit on the moor, organised by a few people for the children but now there is this treat in the village.

I have a weakness for bonfires and fireworks, and sparklers sum up my pleasure. They are magically beautiful, showering their harmless stars in the dark and looking like radiant dandelion clocks. The tangy smell of a burnt-out one is the essence of all fireworks.

The chosen site for the bonfire is roped off in the field and day by day the boxes and planks and branches pile up. It is an excellent way of getting rid of junk, but I often long to extricate some of the wood secretly and put it in my garden shed.

Then, on the day, the fun begins early. The ponies have to come in, for safety's sake. Their stables are put ready, and buckets of tempting goodies are waiting. Last year there were only two of them to catch – Ben and his friend Ted. It took over an hour. Ted was amenable and followed his bucket quite happily, but not so my Ben. He hadn't been stabled since the late spring, and threw forty fits at the idea. It took three of us to get him out of his field, after he had raced up and down and from corner to corner a dozen times, with mane and tail flying.

Once out, he shot into the car park and dodged round that for a bit. Then we fetched Ted out again and paraded him up and down for encouragement, and eventually Ben decided to call it a day and scuttled round to his stable with a wickedly rolling eye, just to keep us on edge that he might scoot off up the road at the last minute, Yes, getting Ben in can be a traumatic experience.

The fireworks, when they are let off, are splendid affairs, and I shudder to think what they cost nowadays. There are all the old faithfuls – the golden rains, the silver fountains, the catherine wheels and the Roman candles. There are modern ones for today's children – sputniks and the like. There are rockets that have two and three cascades of falling stars, and there are the rockets of the grand finale. These are huge, and are let off at five-minute intervals, with loud bangs, zooming over the village to shower us with a final starry glitter.

When it is all over, Patch creeps out from under the bed, stops shivering, and gets into her basket. She hates Bonfire Night. And I love it.

All the local pubs have pool and darts teams, and this is a social world in itself. Non-playing wives and girlfriends go along too, and only really bad weather calls a halt to it. The hazards, on the open moorland roads, are fog and snow. Even a relatively light fall can make a one-in-four hill dangerous, and a breakdown on an exposed bit of road in the dark is a very nasty experience.

There used to be a branch of the British Legion here, and their annual dinner was held every autumn at the pub, followed by a dance. I went as a guest a couple of times. The M.C. for both evenings was a farmer, who looked so different – and less at ease – in his dark suit. When he rose to announce the toasts, his normally rubicund face turned a brighter red, and true British embarrassment at standing up and speaking in public made his voice come out with a strangled tonsils effect.

A day out in the open air gives me a good appetite, which these farmers trebled. Again and again the empty dishes went back into the kitchen, to reappear piled high with golden "roasties". I'll say this for North Devon catering – the food is mouth-watering and the quantities over-flowing. In the days when I stayed in farmhouses, one breakfast would last me all day.

The Legion Dinner is another of those local events which are no more. The membership dwindled away, and the branch ceased. So, too, has a little ceremony which its members kept every year on Remembrance Sunday. This alternates in the valley between two churches, and each year the men would stand outside before the service, wearing their war medals. One of the most senior of them would give the command, and the line would come to attention before they filed into church, to sit together as a group.

There was something touching in the sight. Grey heads and bald heads now, and stooping shoulders where once there had been young men, called away from homes and farms and families to face who knew what? How dear those green fields of England must have seemed to eyes grown weary of foreign sand and dust and mud.

Each year a poppy wreath is placed for those who didn't come back. In a small community, these sad gaps are all the more noticed; I hope we shall never cease to keep Remembrance Sunday. It is like a wind that suddenly rises and stirs the grass, refreshing the memory of events and names that might otherwise be gradually forgotten.

A singsong at one of the local pubs can be a crowded, hot, and boisterous occasion, summer or winter, and if there is a live group playing it can be very noisy. One farmer is notorious for arranging his own singsongs; the landlord gets in his special brown ale, and the locals turn up in force. Will might be persuaded to sing one of the old Exmoor songs which still survive. Sometimes things may descend to the bawdy, as one old man succumbs to the calls for his strip-tease act. I can't think of anything more repulsive than the sight, and the better landlords won't permit it. But that's part of the local way of having “a good night out.”

As the year draws towards its end, the carol singing season starts. We are not plagued in the village by two shrill lines of "While Shepherds watched”, followed by a thump on the door. We have a large and cheerful group, organised by Susan for the past twenty-five years. The members change, but the custom persists, and a charity benefits by over £80 each year. I have been out with them several times, and it is good fun as well as hard work.

Throats get refreshed halfway through the evening at one house or another, where the carol singers are welcomed in to hot punch and mince pies. Then the host and hostess get a carol, perhaps by candlelight, and off we go again to the last houses. The round always finishes at Aunty Ida’s, where tea and coffee, cakes and sausage rolls and sandwiches are liberally supplied. The special warmth of Christmas flows freely, and there is a happy atmosphere as tired feet (and voices) finally wend their ways home.

In recent years, I have chosen to stay home and be one of those visited and sung to; with all the holiday homes and people gone away for Christmas, these seem to get fewer every year. (That is my excuse for not braving a chilly night out of doors!)

I once answered the door to the singers while nursing Toddles, my guinea pig. Sometimes Sam has to be restrained from seizing the chance to flit off in the dark. Patch, who explodes at the first opening bars, has to be hustled into the kitchen, where she kicks up a row until the carol singers go on their amused, good-natured way. Last year they were accompanied by a dog, whose ears shot up, but fortunately he declined to make it a canine duet.

The social round can sometimes spring a lovely surprise. It was in Nolly's time that the last one occurred. He called in one evening to say that a world-famous organist, was giving a recital, which he did from time to time as this where his mother still lived. Two of us were lucky enough to get tickets, and we had a wonderful evening.

Nobody likes to get older, and the goal posts of what counts as old age get moved further ahead every year, as far as I'm concerned.

# Changes

"We haven't been here for five years, and it's just the same." Visitors tell me this when I meet them strolling about. But how wrong they are! When I look back, I am amazed at the changes which have taken place since I bought the cottage. They happen all the time.

Only five houses are now still in the same hands, and five new ones have been built. This summer, two other properties have changed hands again three more are up for sale. A complete wood has been cut down, and another, now owned by the National Trust, has been drastically thinned. Not long ago, a local farm was sold. A large workshop has been built down the road. The pub has been painted, and the long frontage is now black and white instead of royal blue and cream. The shop has closed down. Eighteen familiar faces are no more. Through the valley, a whole generation has passed away, and now the children of some who have gone are, in one case, suddenly not "the Rickerts boys" anymore, but middle-aged men, and beginning to go grey.

I can look up at the trees and shrubs I planted years ago, and the back wall of the cottage is completely covered by the variegated ivy which I stuck in as a 10p throw-out. The house corners are hidden by climbers, and I find it hard to visualise things as they used to be. I wish I were a photographer, because then I might have a more detailed record of the changes, rather than a few snaps here and there which friends have taken. I once enjoyed looking through a "Book of the House" which was a pictorial record of one built at Mullion in Cornwall, starting with the bare site. I wish I'd copied this idea. You think you will remember – but you won't.

And what of the future? "Coming events cast their shadows before them", but I haven't heard of anything startling on the grape vine. Eva's son has just married his girlfriend of long-standing. There is to be another change of incumbent at the church up the valley.

But when people say "it hasn't changed," I know what they mean. There is a feeling of stability about a village in a valley, such as this one is. The hills fold round it in a timeless embrace, speaking of something eternal, as do mountains, rivers and seas. The sun continues to rise at the eastern end of the valley, and sets over the woods in the west, followed by the moon, and in the velvet night, the stars wheel in the patterns we are accustomed to seeing.

As the seasons change and the year moves through its calendar of events, one gets a glimpse of the vast panorama of history, reaching far back into the mists of time. Men have been here for a long, long time, ploughing, sowing, reaping, and wondering, perhaps, about those who will come after them when their day is done. When I walked on the moors this afternoon, and looked at their sweeping curves carved against a sky of Exmoor blue, I thought how lucky I was to be here, in my turn.

There was a faint edge of coolness in the wind, reminding me that summer is slipping away, that before the fragile beauty of another spring, there is a winter to be endured. After this year's poor summer, it seems as if it will come early. There has already been a freak tinge of ground frost, and a gale has wrecked tall plants. Two years ago, there were mushrooms everywhere; this year I haven't picked one. Blackberries, which can hang like grapes, are hard to find but it has been a bumper year for honey.

It is calculated that about 220 million swallows migrate annually. Our first ones left the village very early, between August 16th and 18th, And those still here are much diminished in number, and swirling agitatedly about, obviously wanting to be off.

Robbie has gone; she didn't reappear after the start of the nesting season, and I miss her. Two robins are now battling out the ownership of my garden, a thin one and a fat one. I think the fat one is the same bird who took a crumb from my fingers while still a speckled baby. He or she fluttered across my face once or twice, just as Robbie used to do, and I hope that this one wins, for I have convinced myself that it is one of her blood.

Scraggledy hasn't appeared for breakfast for some time, but the farmer assures me that all is well. She is somewhere "out over", as there's plenty of grass about, but she'll be back, and she is reserved for me in her old age. Sid comes instead, still occasionally stamping, but sociable now, and eating from my hand. "My boys" are still there, as are all the other members of my flock, including Hedgehog; his appetite is dwindling daily, so hibernation will soon set in. I hope he chooses my garden for it again this year.

Little changes but set against the wheel of life, I see them not so much as changes but as different aspects of one great whole. Even the comings and goings in the village are changeless, in a way. We come, and have our day, and when we go it is but to make way for someone else. It is like the dawn, no two ever alike, yet it is the dawn just the same… pearly grey, or rose and gold, or flaming scarlet, a changing part of the changeless.

So, when visitors say to me that things are just the same, I am able to agree, and disagree, with them. A leaf falls... but it has left next year's bud of spring behind. The river hastens by... but millions of drops forever renew it. The wind rises... but beneath it the voice of silence waits to be heard. The village swallows go... but there will be swallows here again next year, in another springtime.

God speed, little travellers.

*THE END…*

The previous page was the end of Liz's book but not the end of the story.

Liz stopped drafting the manuscript for the book in 1996, but despite appointing a literary agent was unable to find a publisher. She continued to live in her beloved cottage until she passed away in 2020 at the age of 93, by this time little had changed from the life she had described: A telephone had been installed, the TV signal now came via a satellite dish and I did manage to get her to accept a new color TV and a monitored personal alarm but she steadfastly refused a washing machine and grew most of her own vegetables using the plastic bottles and guttering method she described until the end of her life.

I knew Liz through my late father Peter, they were cousins, and had grown up together in an area of Bristol called Henleaze during WW2.

Liz trained as a teacher at Redland Training College in Bristol and at the University of Bristol. She taught at Whitehall Junior school in Bristol from 1957 and in 1960 she went to complete a course in Child Development at the University of London before ultimately taking up a post as Head Teacher back in Bristol.

It was during her time as a school head that, in 1971 she purchased Riverside cottage in Brendon. From then on her work pattern was that on Friday night, when school finished she would drive down and spend the weekends enjoying the tranquility of Exmoor returning either on the Sunday evening or early on the Monday morning to her duties.

Retirement enabled her to move full-time to Brendon and she began to write for magazines both short stories and factual pieces many of which were extracts from this book. I had occasionally helped her account for her literary earnings on her tax return and was aware that she had once tried to write this book about her life at the cottage but had not seen it.

Liz continued to drive into her early 80s until suffering a minor stroke in 2012. It fell to me to persuade Liz that she needed to go to hospital and receive treatment, to say she was reluctant would be an understatement. But she eventually agreed after she'd made me promise to go and rescue her if she deemed it necessary.

Liz did indeed deem it necessary to be rescued and was insistent on discharging herself. So, with some apprehension I drove to the hospital in Bideford collecting a variety of medical equipment on the way. I was worried about the reception I would get from the staff at the hospital, in fact the staff couldn't have been more enthusiastic to discharge her, and it later occurred to me that I was perhaps not so much rescuing Lizzie, as is rescuing the staff!

Liz made a great recovery and was soon able to walk unaided to the nearby Staghunters Inn on a Tuesday for her favorite meal of fish pie and Exmoor Ale. She continued to have letters published in garden magazines and frequently won the weekly prize for the best letter; in one to an amateur gardening magazine she described how she had configured the garden following her stroke to make it easier to manage.

My father by now had passed away and Liz was left as the Elder Statesperson of the family, and I found myself as Liz's next of kin. The frequency of my visits increased and I too fell in love with the Exmoor countryside; my drive took me through Porlock and up that famous hill. At the top the rumble noise the car made as it went over the cattle grid next to the AA box 137 at Pitcombe Head seemed to signal an entrance to a different world, a world where sheep and ponies wandered the roads, valleys filled with mist and nature was in charge.

*Liz continued to enjoy the Staghunters Inn, here celebrating her 90th birthday with the next 3 generations of family.*

On my visits we discussed current affairs, gardening and all manner of things and enjoyed many meals together either at the Staghunters Inn or at another of her favorites, the Pavilion in Lynemouth. On my last visit, to deliver a new garden bench, the Covid 19 pandemic was raging, and we did our best to socially distance and I recall that Liz had prepared for lunch her signature dish of a homemade quiche with new potatoes, pulled from the garden that morning and of course freshly picked tomatoes.

We would have regular phone calls on a Sunday evening and the week following the bench delivery she rang to say that when she had been cutting down a small tree with a hand saw a neighbor had noticed her and came around with a chainsaw to finish the job for her which she was very grateful.

One night, the call came not from Liz but from the alarm control room and they said there was an ambulance crew with Liz as were her remarkable neighbours. It had been another stroke but this time much more severe.

Liz had said that she wanted me to have the cottage and true to her word Riverside and its contents were left to me in her will alongside generous bequests to a range of animal charities. Liz had written me detailed instructions for looking after the cottage in an old school exercise book. This covered which tradesmen to use and even where to buy the bird food (Mole Valley Farmers at South Molton ). Also waiting for me on her writing desk was an old carboard box containing the manuscript for this book together with the handwritten notes and draft layouts which have enabled this book to be now published.

In choosing to publish it I am not expecting large numbers of readers but as the book has come together, I have learned a great deal not just about Liz but about the choices one makes in life. I was particularly taken with a line on page 198 "there might not be a tomorrow".

Liz went on to live a full and varied life in which she enhanced the lives of others and helped countless animals. She had a deep understanding of literature, history and human nature and was able to maintain a simple cheerful lifestyle that eludes so many people today. My hope is that perhaps someone reading this book will be helped by Liz's story to find their own path through life.

To finish the story Riverside cottage did again need restoration, the electrics were beyond repair and regulations had moved on a long way from 1971. The chapters in the book about the cottage were very helpful in preparing me for what would be found when I took down the hardboard and when I read how she had found the stones and built the fireplace herself, any thoughts I had been harboring of installing a wood burner quickly diminished.

Liz was way ahead of her time in being Eco friendly, and I felt it was important to respect this and fully insulate the cottage whilst keeping as much of the Victorian character of the cottage and garden as possible, and of course the jar of glass pebbles from the days of beachcombing pictured on page 10, which I intend to add to in time.

I have to confess I have sneaked in some modern appliances, a washing machine and tumble drier, which I think Liz might forgive me for but I am sure the dishwasher and microwave would be regarded as an unnecessary extravagance.

Outside the original patio area to the rear has been restored and the traditional cottage garden preserved and I hope future visitors to the cottage will enjoy the garden and its produce and be able to see and understand how the cottage and its garden continues to represent a wonderfully contented and sustainable way of life, a symbiotic relationship between man, plant and nature. I hope guests will pick and use the flowers, herbs, berries and fruit in the garden and compost what is left.

Riverside cottage is now once again a weekend and holiday home and restoring it has given me an ever deepening understanding of the special place that is Exmoor. I share Liz's belief that the cottage, is not just a home but has its own identity and a life of its own and I hope Liz's book and my contribution in this last chapter tell something of the story of the first 200 years of the cottage.

When not being used by the family it is available to rent through various websites with bookings coming through platforms such as Airbnb or our own website: riversidecottagebrendon.co.uk on which guests have the opportunity to tell the story of their visits through reviews and by this new medium I hope the story of Riverside Cottage and life in Brendon will continue to be told.

~ Nick Ball

*I grew up being told of the prewar adventures of Liz, her brother and my father as children growing up in Bristol. It has been a joy having Liz with us into her 90's and very special that she was able to meet a further 3 generations of the family. The cottage, now restored, is able to host this new generation and I can only wonder what stories Huck, Blake and Bramble will tell and how their memories of Liz and her love of nature will influence them.*

# Dedication And Acknowledgements

Liz Francis first visited and fell in love with Exmoor in her early 20's she went on to buy and restore a Victorian cottage in Brendon and live there for the rest of her life. On her passing the manuscript for this book was waiting for me on her desk. Within it was a letter from the Royal National Lifeboat Association accompanied by an article from the Lifeboat Magazine dated 1st November 1899 which is reproduced on pages 87-88. We are very grateful to the RNLI for this support. Liz commented that many of the lifeboat crew named in the article still had descendants living locally. I am in no doubt that the same spirit of Exmoor folk that propelled the lifeboat on its famous journey to help others also remains. During her time at Riverside Cottage Liz was active in village life and an enthusiastic volunteer with the church and local charities, but when, in old age, her own health deteriorated her friends and neighbours showed to her that same spirit of Exmoor folk; they took her shopping or brought supplies to her and provided the support for her to maintain her independent way of life. This book is dedicated to her friends and neighbours and also all of those Exmoor folk with a spirit of adventure, a sense of humor, and a commitment to caring for each other, now, in the past and in the future.

Printed in Great Britain
by Amazon

22904238R00149